"In a world of one-calorie Christianity and diet discipleship, Arron Chambers issues a clarion call for 'Devotees,' disciples utterly devoted to Jesus. Without this dazzling gem of a book, I never would have properly understood my vocation as devotion."

LEONARD SWEET
Bestselling author, professor (Drew University, George Fox University), and chief contributor to sermons.com

"What a romp! I have rarely enjoyed reading a book as much as I did this one. It was filled with great stories, joyous delight, and powerful meaning. Mary Poppins was right—a spoonful of sugar does help the medicine go down. And what is that medicine? Become a fully devoted follower of Jesus."

BILL HULL
Author of *The Disciple-Making Pastor*, *The Disciple-Making Church*, *Christlike*, and *The Complete Book of Discipleship*

"The mantra of the Christian life is often articulated more like, 'Do More, Be Better, Work Harder' than it is, 'Be Still, Listen, and Follow.' In a world where the faith Jesus invites us into is often twisted into a works- and guilt-driven religion, *Devoted* guides us back toward finding rest in the ways of Jesus."

CHUCK BOMAR
Pastor of Colossae Church in Portland, OR, and author of *Losing Your Religion* and *Better Off Without Jesus*

"Arron's engaging, easygoing style and biblical viewpoint in *Devoted* show me that loving Jesus is not about checking off a religious to-do list. It begins with exploring the depth of His love for me. *Devoted* is a practical, down-to-earth unveiling of the beauty and simplicity of the gospel."

RON BLOCK
Banjoist/guitarist/songwriter/vocalist with Alison Krauss and Union Station

"Arron Chambers has done it again. His writings always teach me truth, hold my attention, and challenge me to become more intentional about my relationship with Jesus Christ. Arron Chambers loves Jesus, and Arron helps me to know and love Jesus more."

DAVE STONE
Pastor of Southeast Christian Church, Louisville, KY

"What I love most about Arron Chambers is his raw transparency and honesty about what it means to follow Jesus. That's why *Devoted* isn't a step-by-step plan to discipleship, but a devotee's journal of the journey to loving Jesus. *Devoted* is a great starting place for any new (or growing) Jesus follower."

GEOFF SURRATT
Pastor and author of *Ten Stupid Things that Keep Churches from Growing*

DEVOTED

ISN'T IT TIME TO FALL MORE IN LOVE WITH JESUS?

ARRON CHAMBERS

NAVPRESS

A NavPress resource published in alliance
with Tyndale House Publishers, Inc.

NAVPRESS⬤®

NavPress is the publishing ministry of The Navigators, an international Christian organization and leader in personal spiritual development. NavPress is committed to helping people grow spiritually and enjoy lives of meaning and hope through personal and group resources that are biblically rooted, culturally relevant, and highly practical.

For more information, visit www.NavPress.com.

Copyright © 2014 by Arron Chambers. All rights reserved.

A NavPress resource published in alliance with Tyndale House Publishers, Inc.

NAVPRESS and the NAVPRESS logo are registered trademarks of NavPress, The Navigators. Absence of ® in connection with marks of NavPress or other parties does not indicate an absence of registration of those marks.

TYNDALE is a registered trademark of Tyndale House Publishers, Inc.

ISBN 978-1-61291-637-8

Cover design by Nicole Grimes

Cover illustration by Dean H. Renninger

Published in association with The Blythe Daniel Agency, Inc., P.O. Box 64197, Colorado Springs, CO 80962.

Unless otherwise identified, all Scripture quotations are taken from *The Holy Bible, English Standard Version*® (ESV®), copyright © 2001 by Crossway, a publishing ministry of Good News Publishers. Used by permission. All rights reserved. Scripture quotations marked NIV are taken from the Holy Bible, *New International Version,*® *NIV.*® Copyright © 1973, 1978, 1984, 2011 by Biblica, Inc.® Used by permission of Zondervan. All rights reserved worldwide. www.zondervan.com. Scripture quotations marked KJV are taken from the *Holy Bible*, King James Version.

Some of the anecdotal illustrations in this book are true to life and are included with the permission of the persons involved. All other illustrations are composites of real situations, and any resemblance to people living or dead is coincidental.

Cataloging-in-Publication Data is Available.

Printed in the United States of America

20	19	18	17	16	15	14
7	6	5	4	3	2	1

And they *devoted* themselves to . . .

— Acts 2:42 (emphasis added)

To My Siblings, Leigh-Angela Holbrook,
Leslie Wood, & Adam Chambers . . .
Devotees, all.
I love how you love Jesus.

CONTENTS

A WORD BEFORE

BEFORE YOU READ any further, I need you to know that you have two options right now.

First option: You can ignore what I'm saying here and jump right into this book. That's perfectly fine, although I do want you to know as you get started that I wrote study questions for individual or group study to go with each chapter; those are available as a free download on www.DevotedBook.com. The questions are designed to help you experience this book in a more lasting and relevant way. That being said, I hope you'll consider the second option.

Second option: Turn to "The 40-Day Devoted Experience" in the back of this book and allow it to guide you into a deeper relationship with Jesus. I wrote this book with the hope that it will help you fall more in love with Jesus. Falling in love can't be forced. Love must come to us on its own terms and in its own time—that's how healthy relationships work. And it's because I want you to have a healthy relationship with Jesus that I created "The 40-Day Devoted Experience."

I explain the reasoning behind "The 40-Day Devoted Experience" in greater detail in chapter 1, so I won't get into much more here, except to say . . . you are beginning a relationship with Jesus. Don't rush it. Let his love come to you, embrace you, and take you deeper. The guide in the back of the book is not a program to be followed but an encounter to be experienced. I hope you'll choose this option and spend the next forty days falling more in love with Jesus.

INTRODUCTION:
JUST LOVE

———

THIS IS NOT the book I set out to write.

I had a plan for a book on discipleship for new Christians—and for those Christians who wanted a deeper faith—that included "Ten Simple Steps for Becoming a Better Disciple," but the more I tried to digest what it really means to be a disciple of Jesus, the more I couldn't stomach the idea that being a follower of Jesus is about following a "simple" plan.

A plan isn't what drives me to work at the church building each day.

A plan isn't what holds me as I hold the hand of a mother and father who have just lost a young child.

A plan isn't what carried me along on the flood of grief after the death of my father.

A plan isn't what brings tears to my eyes as I sing of my love for God.

A plan isn't what drops me to my knees at the side of my kids' beds each night.

A plan isn't what sends me into the highways and hedges with an invitation from the King for the eternal banquet.

A plan isn't what moves me to move with Jesus, following him wherever he leads.

No, I didn't want to write a book that presented a plan for becoming a disciple of Jesus. I wanted to write a book that infused people with a passion to want a deeper relationship with him.

At Journey Christian Church we have a team of passionate people with whom I work to plan upcoming sermon series. Recently, in a meeting of our leadership team, we were wracking our brains, trying to figure out how to secure more ministry volunteers for our rapidly growing church. We have more open ministry slots than we have ministry volunteers, so we started planning a special Sunday to generate more volunteers and fill those slots. One member of my team suggested we use "Just Do Something" as the theme for the recruitment Sunday. Initially that sounded like a great idea to all of us, but the more we tried to flesh out that idea, the more frustrated I became.

"Wait a second," I said to my team, trying to verbalize what was stirring in my heart. "I think we're missing the point."

I turned to one of the women on my staff. "Tammy, how would you feel if Terry acted like spending time with you was a job?"

"I wouldn't like that very much," she said.

"Of course not," I replied, "because you want Terry to

want to spend time with you. You want Terry to spend time with you because he loves you. You don't want him to 'Just Do Something,' do you?"

"Well, I would like him to mow the yard!" she joked.

"Tammy," I continued, "you just want him to love you because he's your husband, you're his bride, and he loves you."

"Exactly!" she replied.

Exactly.

Jesus simply wants the same. He wants us to serve him, worship him, love him, follow him, and volunteer to change diapers in the nursery—not out of obligation, but out of affection.

Do you know that Jesus wants us to love him?

Hold that thought.

DO YOU KNOW THAT YOU ARE LOVED?

Last week, a woman from my congregation came to my office with a lot of pain and a lot of questions that I couldn't answer—and one that I could.

In a moment of anguish she cried, "What can I do to make God love me more?"

What can we do to make God love us more?

Nothing. He can't love us more than he already does.

John, the disciple whom Jesus loved, wrote, "For God so loved the world, that he gave his only Son, that whoever believes in him should not perish but have eternal life" (John 3:16).

We are "so loved" by God.

You ever been "so loved"?

My daughter's stuffed Simba was "so loved." Ashton—who was about seven at the time—cried all the way home from the Orlando Arena when I returned to the van with the bad news that her Simba was nowhere to be found. That stuffed lion never knew how much it was loved because it never lived.

You've never lived until you know how much God loves you.

John also wrote:

Beloved, let us love one another, for love is from God, and whoever loves has been born of God and knows God. Anyone who does not love does not know God, because God is love. In this the love of God was made manifest among us, that God sent his only Son into the world, so that we might live through him. In this is love, not that we have loved God but that he loved us and sent his Son to be the propitiation for our sins. Beloved, if God so loved us, we also ought to love one another. (1 John 4:7-11)

Love does not begin with us; it begins with God. And the love he has for us is endless.

We can't draw it out of him, and we can do nothing to earn it.

To know God is to know love.

Do you know God loves you? God is devoted to you.

How do I know this? How do I know God loves you and is devoted to you? How do we know that another person loves us?

That question seems like it should be easy to answer, yet I'm having a really hard time answering it.

How do you quantify the unquantifiable? How do you define the indefinable? How do you express the inexpressible?

As I look back now, with more understanding and insight into what my dad gave up for my siblings and me when we were growing up, I know—without a doubt—he loved us, because he demonstrated it through countless sacrifices. While we were still children and incapable of giving him much beyond our love and obedience, he regularly went without lunch so my siblings and I could afford our extra-curricular activities. He taught extra classes and took speaking engagements so we could afford to take vacations. He drove an old yellow Pontiac station wagon (a.k.a. "The Banana") instead of a new, or even slightly new, car so he could keep his kids fed and clothed.

But God shows his love for us in that while we were still sinners, Christ died for us. (Romans 5:8)

Every moment of my life, I've known only a faithful, steadfast love from my mom. She was a shelter to whom I could run with my broken heart, my broken dreams, and Dad's broken car, which I wrecked shortly after his death; I fell asleep at the wheel because I stayed up late talking to my girlfriend at college past curfew. Mom was up when I got home to hug me and let me know it was going to be okay. Mom's love never slumbers.

Know therefore that the LORD your God is God, the faithful God who keeps covenant and steadfast love with those who love him and keep his commandments, to a thousand generations. (Deuteronomy 7:9)

I know my kids love me because they say nice things about me to others.

Because your steadfast love is better than life,
my lips will praise you. (Psalm 63:3)

I know my wife loves me because, through everything, her love has never failed.

The LORD is merciful and gracious,
slow to anger and abounding in steadfast love.
(Psalm 103:8)

Yes, God loves us.

TO KNOW GOD IS TO KNOW LOVE

But what is love?

The Bible teaches us that love is knowing God, because God is love. "So we have come to know and to believe the love that God has for us. God is love, and whoever abides in love abides in God, and God abides in him" (1 John 4:16).

To know God is to know the steadfast love of a Father who protects his anointed one from certain death (see Psalm 52:1). To know God is to know the pursuing love of a Father who will run to you—the Prodigal—the moment you turn your face toward home (see Luke 15:11-32). To know God is to know the boundless love of a Father who will not let anything separate him from his children (see Romans 8:38-39). To know God is to know the saving love of a Father who was willing for his Son to die so that you and I could live (see John 3:16).

But to know God is also to know how to love others. As John wrote, "Beloved, let us love one another, for love is from God, and whoever loves has been born of God and knows God. Anyone who does not love does not know God, because God is love" (1 John 4:7-8).

Are you having a hard time loving your boss? Then you don't really know God. Are you having a hard time loving your next-door neighbor who has the dog that barks all night? Then you don't really know God. Are you having a hard time loving your ex-wife and her new husband? Then you don't really know God. Are you having a hard time loving someone in your church? Then you don't really know God.

To know God is to love him, but to know God is also to love one another.

DO YOU LOVE THE LORD?

Do you love the Lord?

This is the most important question we can answer. I believe discipleship begins with the answer to that question.

Why do I believe that? Well, it's a question Jesus asked of the disciple whose message was going to be the foundation on which the church would be built. It was the question Jesus wanted answered before Peter began his ministry of discipleship.

At key moments in my life, I've confirmed the existence of love through questions:

"Do you want to be my girlfriend? If so, check the 'Yes' box."

"Do you want to go out?"

"Do you want to go to homecoming?"

"Do you want to go to prom?"

"Do you want to go to a movie after devotions?"

"Do you want to get back together?"

"Will you marry me?"

"Do you love Rhonda and take her to be your lawfully wedded wife?"

Questions can confirm love, or at least the intent to love.

Do you love the Lord?

I have to ask. Sometimes the only way to truly confirm whether or not love exists is to ask.

Jesus asked Peter, "Simon, son of John, do you love me more than these?"

Peter answered, "Yes, Lord; you know that I love you."

"Feed my lambs," Jesus commanded.

Again Jesus asked Peter, "Simon, son of John, do you love me?"

"Yes, Lord; you know that I love you," Peter replied.

"Tend my sheep," Jesus commanded.

Yet again, Jesus asked the question that was the most important question that disciple and any disciple can answer before being truly ready to lead sheep: "Do you love me?"

"Lord, . . . you know that I love you," Peter declared with grief taking up residence in his heart.

"Feed my sheep," Jesus commanded before the questions ended and Peter was brought back—full circle—to how it all began, with those two words with which all disciples must reckon: "Follow me" (John 21:15-19).

Before Peter could follow and begin the greatest act of discipleship, Jesus wanted to confirm the existence of love. Jesus wanted to know that Peter was devoted to him, because he was devoted to Peter. Jesus wanted this from his disciple Peter, and I believe he wants the same thing from us. I know it's what I want from the people I disciple.

For too long I've asked new converts to Christianity the wrong questions:

"Are you reading your Bible?"
"Are you going to church services each week?"
"Are you praying?"
"Are you giving your tithes and offerings?"
"Are you serving Jesus?"

But I haven't been asking the one question that was so important to Christ that he asked it of Peter three times: "Do you love Jesus?"

Almost every week at Journey, I ask someone this question: "Do you believe Jesus is the Christ, the Son of the living God?" This is our version of the question Jesus asked Peter at a key point in his ministry: "Who do you say that I am?" (Matthew 16:15), to which Peter replied, "You are the Christ, the Son of the living God" (Matthew 16:16).

I've publicly asked *that* question thousands of times, but until now, I've never publicly asked anybody the question Jesus publicly asked Peter three times: "Do you love Jesus?"

Interesting thing—Jesus strongly commanded the disciples not to tell anyone that he was the Christ (see Matthew 16:20), and he taught that the commandment we should obey most strongly is to "love the Lord [our] God with all [our] heart and with all [our] soul and with all [our] mind"

(Matthew 22:37). Why then do we ask new believers to confess the one thing that Christ commanded his disciples *not* to say and then not ask them to confess the one thing he commanded us to do?

Don't get me wrong. I'm not suggesting that we stop asking people to publicly confess their faith in Christ. The answer to that question has eternal implications. Early in his ministry, Jesus taught that "everyone who acknowledges me before men, I also will acknowledge before my Father who is in heaven" (Matthew 10:32). But Jesus said that the greatest thing we can do is to love him.

How then have we gotten it so wrong?

Both confessions—what we believe about Christ and what we feel toward Christ—are good, essential, and life changing. Peter's confession of love for Christ was as foundational to the church as was his "Great Confession."

The church without the confession of Jesus as the Christ, the Son of the living God, is not the church, but a gathering of delusional heretics. The church without love is a gathering of religious Pharisees. But the church made up of confessing Devotees primarily motivated by a passionate love for Jesus is unstoppable.

What would happen in your church and in your community if, when taking someone's confession of faith, we asked the right questions? "Do you believe that Jesus is the Christ, the Son of the living God, and do you love him?"

Love without faith can still be love, but according to the inspired Word of God, faith without love is not faith at all.

THE DEVOTED ONES

For years I've taught that the book of Acts is a history book, but I now believe I've been wrong. Yes. I know, I know. It *is* a book that contains the history of the church, but as I read Acts umpteen times while preparing to write this book, I became convinced that Acts is really a love letter. The book of Acts details the love of a Savior for this world, the love of disciples for their Teacher, and the love of the church for their Lord.

So that's how we're going to approach this journey together. We're reading a love letter to learn better how to love Jesus.

In the church I serve, we are seeing many people come to Christ. As I write this, we've baptized 210 people so far this year, which creates a really good problem for us: We have a lot of new Christians who need to be discipled. So the leadership team of the church started looking for a good discipleship plan that would help us raise up disciples who were passionately in love with Jesus.

We found some good plans out there, but they were all essentially teaching new Christians the same things: Read your Bible more, pray more, go to church every week, start tithing, tell lost people about Jesus, and don't sin. These are all really good things to do, but we didn't want to give our new Christians a list of to-do items. We wanted to give our new Christians an opportunity to fall more in love with Jesus.

We wanted something more for our new Devotees.

Yes—Devotees.

In the New Testament, the word that is used more than any other word to define followers of Christ is the word *disciple*. And I love that name! I'm a humble but proud disciple of Jesus Christ, and I wish to take nothing away from that biblical term. So let me be very clear here: By referring to followers of Christ as *Devotees* in this book, I am not suggesting that the name *disciple* be discarded. By no means!

That being said, the word *disciple* may carry some baggage with both long-term followers of Christ and new believers. So throughout this book—where appropriate—I will use the term *Devotee* because I believe it most clearly defines the kinds of disciples of Christ I hope to raise up.

The standard definition of a disciple is someone who is a student or follower of a teacher, leader, or philosopher. The word *student* takes my mind to a classroom where I find myself listening to lectures, taking a test for which I'm not prepared, and fighting to stay awake. The word *follower* makes me think of standing in a long line at Walt Disney World, in the hot sun, with a bunch of other people walking slowly and steadily toward a destination that may or may not be truly "magical."

A Devotee, on the other hand, is someone who is a fanatical adherent to an individual or to a system of beliefs.

The word *Devotee* sets my heart on fire! Yes, I am a student and follower of Jesus Christ, but I want so much more than knowledge and proximity to Christ. I want passion for Christ—I want to be a fanatical Devotee!

I'm not preaching against being a student and follower of Jesus. I want to raise up a generation of disciples who are fanatically devoted to Christ.

I want you to reconsider both what it means to be fanatically devoted to Christ and what could happen if we honestly evaluate the process by which most churches "make disciples." Consider a new paradigm: love for Jesus.

Churches all over the country are reporting many new disciples as they implement the ingredients for evangelism I wrote about in my book *Eats with Sinners*. Regularly, I'm contacted by churches that have just finished using *Eats with Sinners* in a church-wide program and want to know, "What now? Do you have anything we can use to disciple all of these new believers?"

For several years I've had to say, "No, not yet."

As I prayerfully considered writing a sequel to *Eats with Sinners*, I became more convinced it needed to be a book that helped new Christ-followers build an intentional relationship with God. In *Eats with Sinners* I defined evangelism as an intentional relationship through which someone is introduced to Jesus. In this book I define discipleship as an intentional relationship through which a Christian helps another Christian fall more in love with Jesus.

A book for disciples that does not contain a plan for being a better disciple, but a plea for all disciples to be better at loving Jesus.

A book for disciples who want to love Jesus more today than they did yesterday.

A book for disciples who prefer affection to obligation and aren't content with a mere plan for becoming a better disciple of Jesus.

A book for disciples who want a deeper relationship with Jesus because they know that true discipleship is not a set of rules to be lived but a Savior to be loved.

A book by a disciple of Jesus who knows that disciples who love Jesus will serve him, follow him, give to him, tell people about him, and live for him—not because they have to, but because they want to.

A book for disciples who want to be as devoted to Christ as he is to us.

A book for disciples who want to be fanatically devoted to Christ.

A book that presents a new paradigm for making disciples: love. Just love.

A book that raises up a generation of disciples who prefer to be called "Devotees."

My friend Mark Scott's youngest daughter, Allison, had been studying the Bible and praying for long periods of time, seeking God's will for her future. Last year, she entered Ozark Christian College not knowing what God wanted her to do with her life and not sure she would stay beyond the first semester.

But over dinner during winter break, she told her parents her desire was now to graduate from Ozark. When they asked what had changed and why she now wanted to stay in school, she boldly proclaimed, "I just love Jesus!" I believe true discipleship is not about what you do; it's about whom you love.

It's not about religion; it's about a relationship with Jesus. It's not about obligation to Christ; it's about affection for Christ. It's not about following a plan; it's about falling more in love with Jesus. It's not about duty; it's about devotion. It's not just about confessing our faith; it's also about confessing our love.

And, it's not about leading new converts through "Ten Simple Steps for Becoming a Better Disciple"; it's about raising up a generation of Devotees who explain each step of faith by boldly proclaiming, "I just love Jesus!"

TRUE LOVE WAITS

And while staying with them he ordered them not to depart
from Jerusalem, but to wait for the promise of the Father.
—*Acts 1:4*

AMANDA SAT WITH ME and my wife late one night on our back porch. She felt like she wasn't pleasing God because she wasn't currently involved in any ministries at church. With tears spilling onto her cheeks, she said, "I feel like I need to be doing more for God."

In a moment, I'll tell you what I told her, but you're going to have to be patient.

I can be very impatient. Stoplights are almost unbearable. Don't send me long e-mails. Get to the point, already! I'm always the first one up on Christmas morning. I have a hard time waiting the two minutes and twenty seconds it takes to make microwave popcorn, so I often pull it out before it's done popping—only to lament the number of unpopped kernels in the bottom of the bowl. If possible, I always use the "Self Checkout" lane at the grocery store and also always get annoyed if I have to wait behind a person who is trying to buy twenty-five items with a check in the "15 Items or Less; Cash Only" lane! I always fast-forward through the previews on the rental DVD so we can get to the movie. I DVR NASCAR races so I can race through the commercials and caution flags, finishing most of the four-hour races in less than an hour. And, I struggle with finishing my wife's sentences for her because I'm trying to move the conversation along.

I know, I know. That's not just really annoying; it's also not conducive to a healthy relationship with my wife or anyone else for that matter.

One of the hallmarks of true love is patience.

Hello! The first word from Paul on love is, "Love is patient" (1 Corinthians 13:4).

TRUE LOVE WAITS

To some, the words *True Love Waits* may be nothing more than the tagline of a Christian youth abstinence movement which has been engraved on purity rings, pendants, T-shirts, keys, bracelets, dog tags, visors, journals, Bibles, hoodies, bumper stickers, Christmas tree ornaments, buttons, infant bodysuits, baby bibs, teddy bears, thank-you cards, tote bags, mouse pads, coffee cups, pajamas, boxers, and thongs[1] worn by countless teens and young adults who have pledged to not have sex before marriage, which is a good thing. Not having sex before marriage, that is. Testifying to your vow of premarriage celibacy on the front of your boxers or thong is not necessarily a good thing. At that point you may actually just be testifying that your moral convictions are really only abstract ideas to which you are barely committed and which can be stripped away as easily as your outer garments, revealing words that really don't resonate on polished cotton and lace as well as they resonate when pledged at the altar of a Christian teen convention.

Do you see the irony of wearing undergarments that testify to your belief that "True Love Waits"? The only way for said undergarments to be seen is for someone to not wait on the appropriate side of your boundaries of sexual purity (which doesn't seem to be very loving to you), or for you to compromise your own moral boundaries for the desires of another (which doesn't seem to be very loving to yourself).

If you truly love someone, you will wait.

You will wait so you can walk her home from the bus stop.

You will wait patiently in her living room, making uncomfortable small talk with her dad, as she changes her dress for the tenth time.

You will wait to have sex with her until safely within the covenant of marriage.

You will wait for her at the front of the church in anticipation of the proclamation of sacred promises.

You will wait as he serves our country in a foreign land.

You will wait up, with a candle in your window, so you can kiss him good night when he gets home from work.

You will wait for her to finish her sentences on her own.

You will wait in the surgery waiting room, hoping for news that the cancer hasn't spread.

And, you'll wait in Jerusalem because that's what Jesus said to do.

Are you willing to wait for Jesus?

I don't want you to rush this relationship-with-Jesus thing. Let's take it slowly. Let's be patient. I don't want you to start working for the Lord right now; I want you to start waiting on the Lord right now.

Which is not the course of action we preachers most often encourage in new Christians. What we most often encourage new Christians to do is nothing. You give your life to the Way, and we give you no direction on how best to follow Christ for the next week, let alone for the rest of your life.

Typically, we preachers just let you start doing whatever it is you think new Christians do after their conversion, which typically looks like reading through the Bible from beginning to end, praying twenty-four hours a day, giving all of your money to starving kids in Kenya, joining a small group, and going to church every time the doors are open. In my experience, these activities by new Christians rarely last very long because they are a lot of work.

And, if we do "do something" to give you some direction after your conversion, it usually looks like this. Before you've even dried off the waters of the baptistery, we hand you a Bible, a Certificate of Baptism (a document necessary for admission to heaven), a schedule of our Sunday school classes, and a directory of our small groups—and if we're really on the ball, we hand you a copy of *The Purpose Driven Life*, pat you on the back appropriately, and send you on your way down the uneventful and completely trouble-free road to eternal glory.

As I've fallen more and more in love with Jesus and become more devoted to him, I've become more convicted that the best thing to do at the beginning of a relationship with Jesus is to do what Jesus did at the beginning of his ministry and what the disciples were commanded to do at the beginning of their ministries: Wait.

After his baptism in the Jordan River, Jesus was led by the Holy Spirit into a wilderness for forty days. Jesus waited forty days after his baptism to begin his ministry. During this time he fasted, prayed (fasting was always accompanied by prayer), and was tempted by the Devil.

This is so atypical of what we preachers model and expect of new Christians. If we'd been running the show (so to speak), we would have had Jesus get right to work as soon as he dried off and changed clothes after his baptism.

"The clock is ticking!"

"You gotta make hay while the sun is shining!"

"You've got to strike while the iron's hot!"

"Today is the day of salvation!"

"The salvation of a lost world is at stake, so we'll have none of this taking forty days off to wait upon your Father right after your baptism."

Which is why so many new Christians flame out too soon.

Do you know what Jesus didn't do after his baptism?

He didn't go to the synagogue for over a month.

He didn't pay a single tithe.

He didn't take a new believers' class.

He didn't read from the Torah.

He just followed the Holy Spirit into a time of waiting.

The salvation of a lost world is at stake, so you better take forty days to wait upon the Lord after your baptism.

Do you see how bizarre this is, in light of what we typically expect from new Christ-followers? This is the opposite of what we consider to be true discipleship. I think there'd be considerable resistance in the typical church if the pastor expected people to follow Christ's example.

"Congratulations on giving your life to Christ and being baptized! Now, here's what we want you to do. We want you to not go to church for the next forty days. We don't want you to pay a dime toward your tithe. We don't want you to sign up for our New Believers' Class. We don't want you to read your Bible. We just want you to follow the Holy Spirit into a season of waiting."

For so many of us—and by "us," I mean Christian leaders and people who have spent decades in the church—this does not fit into the paradigm we call "discipleship."

We Christians, convicted that "now is the day of salvation" (2 Corinthians 6:2), have convinced ourselves that, in most situations, waiting is a waste of time, and when it comes to our faith walk, waiting is almost sinful. But these beliefs are nonsense, unbiblical, and toxic to developing a healthy and lasting relationship with Jesus.

The Bible is replete with faithful people who had to wait faithfully.

God promised Noah, "I will establish my covenant with you, and you shall come into the ark, you, your sons, your wife, and your sons' wives with you" (Genesis 6:18). But Noah had to wait probably twenty to forty years for this promise to be realized.

Abraham was seventy-five years old when God first promised him, "And I will make of you a great nation, and I will bless you and make your name great, so that you will be a blessing. I will bless those who bless you, and him who dishonors you I will curse, and in you all the families of the earth shall be blessed" (Genesis 12:2-3). But Abraham and Sarah had to wait twenty-five more years for the birth of Isaac.

Joseph was only seventeen when God gave him a dream revealing that his brothers would bow down before him (see Genesis 37:1-11). But he had to wait about twenty-four years, enduring thirteen years in Potiphar's house and in prison and seven years of famine, before his prophetic dreams were fulfilled.

The children of Israel waited in the silence of God for about four hundred years in Egypt before he responded and sent Moses to deliver them. They then waited for forty years in the wilderness before finally being released into the Promised Land.

King David, while waiting under the threat of adversaries and "false witnesses," testified, "Wait for the LORD; be strong, and let your heart take courage; wait for the LORD!" (Psalm 27:14).

Hannah desperately wanted a son, so she prayed and waited faithfully for years and years before God finally answered her prayer "in due time" with Samuel (1 Samuel 1:20).

When the people of God were waiting for deliverance during a time of intense trials during the reign of King Ahaz, the prophet Micah testified, "But as for me, I will look to the LORD; I will wait for the God of my salvation; my God will hear me" (Micah 7:7).

Prophesying of the time when God's people would be held captive in Babylon, Isaiah promised, "Even youths shall faint and be weary, and young men shall fall exhausted; but they who wait for the LORD shall renew their strength; they shall mount up with wings like eagles; they shall run and not be weary; they shall walk and not faint" (Isaiah 40:30-31). Isaiah also said, "From of old no one has heard or perceived by the ear, no eye has seen a God besides you, who acts for those who wait for him" (Isaiah 64:4).

The author of Lamentations (probably Jeremiah the prophet) reminded the people of God, after the fall of Jerusalem, "The LORD is good to those who wait for him, to the soul who seeks him. It is good that one should wait quietly for the salvation of the LORD" (Lamentations 3:25-26).

Rewards, strength, and salvation are all promises tied to waiting on the Lord, so we should not be surprised that Jesus was led by the Holy Spirit into a forty-day period of waiting before beginning his ministry.

And we should not be surprised that before the apostles began their ministry in Jerusalem, Jesus appeared to them for a period of about forty days and ordered them to stay in Jerusalem "to wait for the promise of the Father" (Acts 1:4).

WAITING IS THE HARDEST PART

We want results and we want them now and we want them to come without a great deal of effort.

Spend some time watching late-night TV, and you'll see what I mean. The late-night airwaves are saturated with a constant stream of resources, plans, and gadgets that will improve your life immediately, satisfaction guaranteed (or you'll get your money back, in sixty to ninety days).

If you feel like thirty seconds is too long to open your can of soup with an "old-fashioned" hand-crank can opener, the Tornado Can Opener is an answer to your prayers! It will open your cans in twenty-five seconds!

Think that it takes too much time to clean your ears with a cotton swab? No worries! WaxVac will clear the wax out of your ears quicker than a cotton swab ever dreamed of!

Forget going to the barbershop or hair salon. Trimming your hair now takes only seconds with Micro Touch Max!

Want fantastic abs? Forget those silly crunches and sit-ups! The Ab Rocket will give you great abs in just five minutes a day! Plus, it comes with the Fat Blasting System! Blast your fat into cellulite oblivion with minimal effort and even less sweat!

Want to transform your entire body in fewer than sixty days? Then you'd be crazy not to try the INSANITY Workout!

If that doesn't work, you can wear the Slim Away girdle and you'll look slimmer instantly!

And, if that doesn't work, you can join the countless others who spend $1.2 billion[2] annually just to have your fat sucked away in only moments . . . while you sleep!

I don't know if you've realized it, but exercise is hard work.

Well, so is waiting, which is why Jesus had to order the apostles to stay and to wait (see Acts 1:4).

STOP, IN THE NAME OF LOVE!

Do you know who else needs to be ordered to "stay" and wait? My two Labrador retrievers! My cat, on the other hand, ignores any and all orders, but that's another story for an article I'm writing on eschatology entitled "Welcome to Hell! Here's Your Cat!"

Animals aren't known for their self-control. Neither are immature Christians.

Self-control is one of the fruits of the Spirit and is also evidence of true devotion to Jesus.

Jesus, knowing the human propensity for chasing after cars, orders his followers to follow him in waiting for forty days before beginning their ministries.

But why wait?

Why did Jesus wait forty days before preaching the gospel in Nazareth? Why did the apostles wait fifty days before preaching the gospel in Jerusalem? Why am I about to order . . . ask . . . beg you to wait forty days before you do anything else?

Because I want you to have a relationship with Jesus.

Because I want you to be strong.

Because I want you to have a strong relationship with Jesus.

Do you know that the Law of Moses required a newly married soldier to be relieved of duty for a year so he could spend time with his wife?

When a man is newly married, he shall not go out with the army or be liable for any other public duty. He shall be free at home one year to be happy with his wife whom he has taken. (Deuteronomy 24:5)

Why did God command this of a newly married man? Because God understands relationships more than we ever could, and he wanted Israelite marriages to be strong. The first year of marriage is crucial to the long-term stability and strength of the relationship, so it was important that the new couple spend uninterrupted time together. This phase of the relationship—this period of inaction and waiting—was a God-ordained opportunity to strengthen the relationship and guarantee future fruitfulness.

Inaction, for the Devotee of Christ, is not a sign of weakness but an opportunity for strength. Waiting, for the Devotee of Christ, is not a sign of unfruitfulness but the only way to be truly fruitful.

I believe one of the reasons the apostle Paul was used in such a dynamic way to help people see the truth was because he had to wait. After encountering God in a transformational way on the road to Damascus, he was forced into a three-day period of waiting in blindness before he was released into his ministry (see Acts 9:9).

Jesus wanted the apostles to be fruitful, so he ordered them to wait for something very specific: the promise of the Father. What promise was God going to give them if they were willing to wait?

Wait for it.

Wait for it.

Power, in the person of the Holy Spirit.

Jesus promised that if they would stop and wait in Jerusalem, at just the right time and in just the right way the Father would give them all of the power they were going to need to do everything they were going to be called upon to do.

Power.

Do you feel powerful? Any physical trainer will tell you that you don't get more powerful sitting around and doing nothing. I'm not your physical trainer, and I could not care less how much you can lift, how far you can run, and how many trans fats you ate today. I only care about one thing right now: Do you love Jesus?

Do you love him enough to stay? "And while staying with them he ordered them not to depart from Jerusalem" (Acts 1:4).

Do you love him enough to wait for him? "But to wait for the promise of the Father" (Acts 1:4).

Do you love him enough to wait for him to speak to you? "He said to them . . ." (Acts 1:7).

Do you love him enough to wait for him to empower you? "But you will receive power when the Holy Spirit has come upon you" (Acts 1:8).

Do you love him enough to wait for him to direct you? "And you will be my witnesses in Jerusalem and in all Judea and Samaria, and to the end of the earth" (Acts 1:8).

In his book *A Thousand Splendid Suns,* Khaled Hosseini writes, "Of all the hardships a person had to face, none was more punishing than the simple act of waiting."[3]

Waiting for a call to see if you got the job.

Waiting for payday.

Waiting for your son to return from his tour of duty overseas.

Waiting for the positive pregnancy test and then waiting for the birth.

Waiting for the doctor to come out and tell you how your father's surgery went.

Waiting for the results of the biopsy.

Waiting can be punishment, but in my experience it's easier to endure hardships while one waits if what is desired is worth the wait.

As we begin this journey together, I'm not asking you to take another step.

I'm not asking you to sign up for a 101 class. I'm not

asking you to start reading through the Bible so you can finish by the end of the year. I'm not asking you to take a spiritual-gifts inventory. I'm not asking you to join a small group. I'm not asking you to sign up for the next mission trip to Mexico. I'm not asking you to volunteer for the third shift in the nursery.

Over the next forty days, God may ask you to do some, or all, of these things—but I won't.

It's like a honeymoon. The honeymoon is an important time in a marriage relationship. It's where a couple starts to really get to know each other in an emotional, physical, spiritual, and biblical sense.

Yes, I just said "biblical" sense. Let me remind you about this verse from Genesis: "Now Adam knew Eve his wife, and she conceived and bore Cain" (Genesis 4:1). The word *knew* in this verse (*yada* in Hebrew) means "to have sexual intercourse." During the honeymoon period of a marriage, a couple takes their relationship to a new level by getting to "know" each other. Intimacy breeds strong relationships.

I'm asking you to put down your sword, go home, and get to know your new spouse.

I'm asking you to view this stage of your relationship with Jesus as a honeymoon period.

I'm asking you to enter into a God-ordained opportunity to strengthen your new relationship with Christ with the hopes that this time of waiting will guarantee future fruitfulness.

I'm asking you to do what I asked Amanda to do when she said, "I feel like I need to be doing more for God."

When, through tears, Amanda wondered what "more" she needed to "do" to be more pleasing to God, I echoed the words scripted by the psalmist, sung by the saints of old, and soothing to the devoted soul, "Be still, and know that I am God" (Psalm 46:10).

Stay!

Wait.

Be still.

As we begin this journey toward a deeper devotion to Christ, I'm asking you to follow Christ's example and allow the Holy Spirit to guide you into, and through, a forty-day period of waiting.

Follow *The 40-Day Devoted Experience* not out of duty but out of devotion.

Don't be reckless, unfaithful, or unguarded during this period. Remember, Christ endured a direct attack from Satan during his forty days of waiting in the wilderness. Know that Satan wants to break your heart the moment you offer it to Christ.

Keep going to church. Keep praying. Read your Bible. Worship.

Give. Make wise choices. Pay your taxes. Bathe. Show up to work on time. Keep reading this book.

Yet, all the while, be still before the Lord.

I'm not asking you to be disobedient; I'm asking you to be devoted to waiting upon the Lord with the hopes that you will become more devoted to the Lord upon whom you've been waiting.

So what does waiting for the Lord over the next forty days look like? In the stillness of the next forty days, simply follow the example of the apostles in Acts 1.

Love Jesus enough to stay . . . resolved not to move until he says so.

Love Jesus enough to wait for him . . . to show up.

Love Jesus enough to wait for him to speak to you . . . as to his specific plan for your life.

Love Jesus enough to wait for him to empower you . . . for every good work he has prepared for you to do.

Love Jesus enough to wait for him to direct you . . . on how you can fall more and more in love with him.

I've written the rest of this book to facilitate meditation, reflection, and increased devotion over the next forty days. I pray that, as you continue to read through this book, you'll hear clearly from the Lord.

• • •

The relief and release that Amanda experienced at the proclamation of that Scripture was physically evident.

She stopped crying.

She sat up.

She breathed a literal sigh of relief.

She smiled.

"Amanda, do you know that Jesus loves you?" I asked.

"Yes, I do," she replied.

"Amanda," I continued. "Do you love Jesus?"

She paused, smiled sincerely, and said enthusiastically, "Yes, I do."

To which I said, "Then, be still and wait."

In the midst of her pain and confusion, Amanda had forgotten it was okay to wait upon the Lord. Like so many of us, she'd allowed herself to believe that the only way she could truly please the Lord was by doing more work for God.

Somehow she'd missed and forgotten the message so clearly written on the front of the undergarments worn by well-meaning Christian teens and singles from sea to shining sea: *True love waits.*

CHAPTER 2

TRUSTING: OF DEPENDENCY AND DYNAMITE

_____

But you will receive power when the Holy Spirit has come upon you.—Acts 1:8

TRUST IS SACRED.

It's the key ingredient in every healthy relationship. If there is no trust, there is no true love, which is why I know my youngest son, Sylas, truly loves me.

A few years ago, I was standing by the front door of our house, with my back to the stairs, talking to some friends and not paying attention to Sylas, who was at the top of the stairs.

Do you know how you sometimes hear something, but it doesn't quite register at first?

"Yes, we had a good time, but I kind of messed up the car. Night, Dad!"

"Honey, I'm so glad that you're finally getting around to

finishing that guest room. My mom will be so happy when she gets here next week."

"This grocery store is always so clean. It's why I drive across town to shop here. Okay, don't forget we need milk. Oh, and dill pickles too. I've been craving dill pickles ever since I found out that I'm pregnant. Oh, we need a box of cereal, too. Are you in the mood for a movie? Let's see if anything good is out."

Well, I had one of those experiences that day with my son.

I was chatting with some friends at my front door when it happened. "So why again are you craving dill pick . . . What?" I yelled in a moment of auditory clarity as I realized that, behind me, my five-year-old son had just yelled, "Catch me, Dad!"

An explosion of adrenaline released from somewhere within me and surged through my core and out to my appendages as I whirled around and extended my arms just in time to catch my son before his toes touched the ground.

Sylas was all giggles and smiles.

I was all . . . needing to change my "True Love Waits" boxers.

My son had launched himself from the safety of the ninth step of our soft, carpeted stairs toward our cold, hard, ceramic tiled floor, expecting me to catch him because he trusts me. Because he loves me.

Love is trust.

Trust is love.

Love is life.

Life is trust.

Trust is life.

We all put our faith in something. At key points throughout our lives we take leaps of faith, expecting something or someone to catch us.

Unless you were delivered by C-section or at home like a scene out of *Little House on the Prairie*, life for most of us begins with one big, "Catch me!" as we're launched, against our wills—screaming and crying—out of the safety of the womb into a cold, hard world and the outstretched arms of, not our dad, but a well-paid masked stranger.

There's a sacred trust in every delivery room. A trust that the weakest person in the room will be clothed, cared for, protected, and nurtured by the most powerful people in the room. A trust that the infant will be caught.

I want infants in Christ to expect to be caught.

I want you to expect to be caught.

I want you to trust that you will be caught.

I want you to take daring leaps, knowing that the loving and dependable arms of your Father await you as you exit the womb, just before your toes hit the ground.

I want you to begin this journey by allowing yourself to become completely dependent on the power of God.

DEPENDENCY

As a pastor, I've made a consistent mistake when welcoming newborn Christ-followers into this world. I've expected them to be too independent too soon.

A baby can't move himself, feed himself, speak for himself, care for himself, comfort himself, or do anything for himself, nor do we expect him to. Imagine how bizarre it would be to hear a new father in the delivery room, only moments after birth, giving the following instructions to a new baby: "Congratulations on your birth! Here's what you're going to need to do right now in order to survive. You're going to need to figure out how to find nourishment, stay clean, get where you need to go, find a home, connect with a family, and—eventually—teach yourself how to walk, speak, think, and live properly. Congratulations, and God bless you!"

What's even more bizarre is that this is how so many Christian leaders treat new Christians, if we do anything at all: "Congratulations on your new birth! Here's what you're going to need to do right now in order to survive. You're going to need to figure out how to find nourishment through God's Word, stay morally clean in this messy sinful world, get where you need to go in your relationship with God, find a church home to attend, connect with a church family or small group, and—eventually—teach yourself how to walk with the Lord, speak the truth, think with the mind of Christ, and live properly as salt and light in this world. Congratulations, and God bless you!"

In an ideal situation, infants aren't expected to do anything. They're just expected to be . . . to trust. Why? Because they are powerless.

Powerlessness is an opportunity to experience a power beyond oneself.

"MY DO IT!"

My daughter Ashton is a strong-willed young woman who was also a strong-willed little girl who once refused my help with riding her bike because she knew that she didn't need me. I can still see the moment so clearly in my mind that it feels like I can reach out once again to try to assist her.

She was two and a half. Hair—blonde and arranged in short ponytails. Eyes—crystal blue and full of sparkles, wonder, and determination. Feet—spinning in the air just above the pedals of her new, pink My Little Pony bicycle. Like all first-time parents, we erred during that first run at parenting by buying gifts prematurely.

You know what I'm talking about, right? You've surely seen the pictures.

Baby boy in a crib with a full-sized football or ball glove.

Baby girl with a boxed collectable Barbie doll in a red velvet dress.

Little militia baby wearing camouflage and lying next to a Mossberg 12-gauge pump action shotgun and a picture of Ronald Reagan.

Adorable blonde two-and-a-half-year-old girl on a pink My Little Pony bike, unable—even with the seat in the lowest position—to reach the pedals.

She was going nowhere.

I wanted to help her go somewhere, so I bent over and said, "Sweetie, let Daddy push you."

Which was met immediately with a defiant, "No! My do it!"

Does it speak less of me as a father that I found pleasure in watching her sit there and flail her legs in a desperate attempt to ride that bike? Does it surprise you that she eventually gave up, gave in, and asked me to help her? Do you know that I wanted her to be dependent on me early in her life so she could go somewhere later in her life?

I just wanted her to hold on and enjoy the ride.

It's a delicate balance, raising kids who are both dependent and independent. I want my kids to know, from their first memories, that they can depend on me. I want them to know that I do what I say I'm going to do, I'll be there when they need me, I'll catch them when they leap in my direction, and my strength is at their disposal.

Children who come into this world and never feel protected quickly come to believe that they can't trust anyone; they can only depend on themselves. Independence becomes their passion; independence becomes their prison.

Freedom without boundaries is an illusion because it's not truly freedom at all.

Disagree? Ask someone who used his freedom to buy and use methamphetamines, but who is now addicted, if he feels free. Ask that young woman who used her freedom to sleep with every guy who showed her some attention, but who now carries an incurable STD, if she feels free. Ask that couple who used their freedom to purchase the American Dream on credit, but who now owes more money than they can ever repay, if they feel free.

Ask my friend Leo, who used his newfound freedom from

prison to rejoin his old gang and rob a grocery store, but who now serves eighteen years in prison, if he feels free.

Leo's situation grieves me. I baptized him last fall, welcomed him and his girlfriend into our small group, rang in the New Year with him, and spent this past winter discipling him. It was during my time of discipleship with Leo that the idea for this book was birthed. I worked through my early visions for this book with Leo, seeking an approach to discipleship that focused on loving Jesus—and he seemed to be getting it.

I asked him, many times, "Do you love Jesus?"

Time after time he enthusiastically replied, "I sure do!"

I worked with some friends to get him a really good job on the oil fields. He needed a safe place to live, far from the reach of the gang, so my wife and I discussed letting him live with us, but—before any of this materialized—Leo was asked by one of his former gang members, "Do you want to help us rob this grocery store?" He enthusiastically replied, "I sure do!"

As I reflected on what went wrong, I realized that Leo was abandoned as a young child. He began living on the streets at age twelve. He learned early on that he could only trust himself. By the age of fifteen, he was living in a home, driving a car, and spending money provided by the gang. Years ago, the gang had found a young boy who didn't think he could trust anyone and convinced him that he could trust only them. Now, since he's rejoined his old gang, I can clearly see the enslaving power of his dependence on the gang and the invisible chains around his heart and mind.

I wish I could get a do-over with Leo. If I could, I'd be

more aware that, even though he declared his love for Jesus, he was still just a baby Christian who hadn't been convinced yet that he could depend on God. Now, his independence is gone.

I wish he'd learned to trust Jesus.

Yes, we can learn to trust Jesus.

How?

By leaping into his arms. By submitting to his power, holding on, and enjoying the ride.

Wanting his disciples to learn to trust him, Jesus said, "Trust me." Well, he didn't say it that way. He said it this way: "It is not for you to know times or seasons that the Father has fixed by his own authority. But you will receive power when the Holy Spirit has come upon you" (Acts 1:7-8).

Knowing them, Jesus knew that they wanted to know "times" and "seasons." They wanted to know where they were going to land and how they were going to have the power to do what he wanted them to do, but he didn't want them to do anything.

As you begin your relationship with Jesus, I don't want you to do anything; I just want you to be . . . to trust. Why? Because you and I are powerless without the power only God can provide. And God will provide all the power you need. Trust me. Trust him.

As a new Christ-follower, you are a spiritual infant. You've been born again. You are a new creation. You have a new name. You have a new family. You've been delivered into a new life . . . a new love. Let this new love come to you, cradle you, care for you, guide you, and empower you. Learn to depend on God. You will grow. You will learn. You will walk. You will flourish. But for now, you must trust. Why? Because you will receive in abundance all the physical and emotional tools you need to do these things. Jesus called it "*power*."

DYNAMITE

In the first chapter of Acts, we see the apostles' ministry beginning with one big "Catch me!" moment as they are launched out of the safety of Christ's physical presence into a cold, hard world where they are called by Christ to live and die for the sake of the gospel.

Yes, Jesus called them to die—if that's what it was going to take—to share his message with the world. However, before he called them to die, he called them to trust that he would provide through the Holy Spirit all the power they were going to need.

But you will receive power when the Holy Spirit has come upon you. (Acts 1:8)

Notice Jesus doesn't say, "You might receive power" or "I sure hope you receive power." He says, "You *will* receive power" (emphasis added).

The word Christ uses in this promise of power is the

Greek word *dunamis*, which is where we get the word *dynamite*.

Do you feel dynamite as you face the challenges you must face today?

Do you feel powerful as you pay your bills?

Do you feel powerful at work?

Do you feel powerful at school?

Do you feel powerful as you face challenges in your relationship with your husband or wife?

Do you feel powerful as you face temptation?

Do you feel powerful as you parent?

Do you feel powerful in the face of your health problems?

Do you feel powerful as you read the headlines today?

Do you feel powerful as you follow Christ today?

Jesus doesn't say that you *will* receive power "when you please me" or "when you are more lovable" or "when you get your act together" or "when you earn it" or "when you stop looking at porn" or "when you start tithing" or "when you lead someone to Jesus" or "when you prove that you can handle the power" or "when you finish reading this book."

We *will* receive power when the Holy Spirit comes on us.

Let's talk about the Holy Spirit.

When I was growing up, and in the church I attended, it seemed we didn't know what to do with the Holy Spirit. We wanted the Holy Spirit to show up late for worship, sit in the back row, wear a disguise, and leave early. We believed in the Trinity: Father, Son, and Holy Spirit. But we mostly talked—and sang—about only the first two entities.

The Holy Spirit was treated kind of like that flamboyant crazy aunt at family gatherings who drives a multi-colored Volkswagen van, wears tie-dyed clothing, and appears to not own a hairbrush or razor. We tolerate her, as long as she agrees to show up late, maintain discretion while with us, and leave our gatherings early. She's not a bad person. No, in fact, she's a very good person. She's a lawyer, a member of the Peace Corps, a bereavement counselor, a marriage counselor, an advocate for the abused, a fantastic teacher, a highly regarded healer, a skilled translator, and the best friend anyone could ever want.

It's not that we don't like her; we just don't know what to do with her. She's just so unpredictable.

She doesn't seem to care anything about the schedule we've so meticulously prepared for our family gatherings. She's loud. Sometimes she starts speaking another language. She talks with her hands (which always seem to be in the air). She loves to dance. She claps. She cries. You can't be in her presence without her trying to touch you. If someone starts to cry, she's the first one to go to that person's side to offer comfort and a clean tissue. In general, she doesn't seem to respect our well-defined social boundaries.

Please, don't be distracted by my picture of the Holy Spirit as a woman. That's not my point. As a matter of fact, the word for *Spirit* is gender-neutral, but on at least five occasions, the pronoun *he* is used in connection with the Holy Spirit (see John 15:26; John 16:7-8,13-14).

My point is that some Christians don't seem to know what to do with the Holy Spirit. They don't get her . . . it . . . him.

It appears some of us are fascinated with, interested in, curious about, but also intimidated by the Holy Spirit, so we tolerate his existence from across the room instead of making eye contact, moving closer, pulling up a chair close to him, embracing him, and asking him if he'd like to take a walk around the block so we can get to know each other better.

As one who has only of late really embraced the Holy Spirit, I need to tell you that he is dynamite and very worth knowing. So let me take a moment to introduce you to the Holy Spirit.

The Holy Spirit Is a Distinct Person

The Holy Spirit is what persons are: a Person to be listened to (see Acts 13:2), a Person who works (see 1 Corinthians 12:11), an intelligent Person (see Isaiah 11:2), and a loving Person (see Ephesians 4:30).

The Holy Spirit does what persons do: he thinks (see Romans 8:27), he knows (see 1 Corinthians 2:10-11), he directs (see Acts 16:7), he speaks (see Acts 13:2), he loves (see Romans 15:30), and he helps (see Romans 8:26).

The Holy Spirit responds as a person: he can be lied to (see Acts 5:3), he can be tested (see Acts 5:9), he can be resisted (see Acts 7:51), he can be grieved (see Ephesians 4:30), and he can be blasphemed (see Matthew 12:31).

The Holy Spirit Is a Divine Person

The Holy Spirit is on a par with God the Father and God the Son (see Matthew 28:19; 2 Corinthians 13:14; 1 Peter 1:2).

The Holy Spirit shares the infinite characteristics of the Deity: he is eternal (see Hebrews 9:14), he is all knowing (see 1 Corinthians 2:10-11), he is everywhere all at once (see Psalm 139:7-12), he is creative (see Genesis 1:1), he is loving (see Romans 15:30), and he is holy (see Acts 2:38).

The Holy Spirit is referred to as "God" in Scripture (Acts 5:4).

The Holy Spirit can be sinned against (see Matthew 12:31; Mark 3:28; Luke 12:10; Acts 7:51; Ephesians 4:30; Hebrews 10:29; 1 Thessalonians 5:19).

The Holy Spirit is a distinct divine person. He is separate from the Son (see John 14:16), and he is distinct from the Father (see Matthew 3:16).

The Holy Spirit Is a Dynamite Person

The Holy Spirit has the power to create this world (see Genesis 1:1; Job 33:4; Psalm 104:30), and he works to sustain life on this planet (see Job 34:14).

In the Old Testament we see the Holy Spirit working in many ways:

- He equipped and empowered people for service: Joseph (see Genesis 41:38), Bezalel and Oholiab (see Exodus 31:1-6; Exodus 35:31-35), Joshua (see

Numbers 27:18), Othniel (see Judges 3:10), Gideon (see Judges 6:34), Jephthah (see Judges 11:29), Samson (see Judges 13:25; 14:6,19; 15:14), and David (see 1 Samuel 16:13).

- He revealed God's person, presence, providence, and plans (see Numbers 11:25-26; 1 Samuel 10:6,10; 1 Chronicles 28:12; 2 Chronicles 24:20; Nehemiah 9:20,30; 2 Peter 1:20-21).
- He was ever present, promoting the providential blessing of God's people (see Genesis 6:3; Joshua 1:8-10; Isaiah 59:21; Haggai 2:5).
- His work was envisioned as expanding in the future (see Isaiah 11:2; 44:3; Ezekiel 36:26,27; Joel 2:28-32).

In the New Testament we also see ways the Holy Spirit was and still is at work:

- He was at work in the incarnation of Christ (see Matthew 1:18; Luke 1:35), in the direction and empowerment of Jesus Christ's earthly life and ministry (see Matthew 3:16; 12:28; Luke 4:1,18; John 1:32), and in the death, burial, and resurrection of Jesus Christ (see Romans 1:4; 8:11; 1 Peter 3:18).
- He poured out essential power on the Day of Pentecost (see Acts 2:1-13) and in preparing the apostles for their foundational role (see Acts 1:8).

- He has the power to produce the Word of God (see John 14:26; 15:26; Ephesians 3:4-5; 1 Timothy 4:1; 2 Timothy 3:16; 1 Peter 1:10-12; 2 Peter 1:21; Revelation 1:10-11).
- He has the power to spread the Word around the world (see Acts 2:1-13; 13:2; 15:28; 16:7), to save and sanctify converts (see John 16:8-11; Ephesians 6:17; 1 Thessalonians 1:5), and to work through the Word of God to bring them to faith (see John 16:8-11; 20:31; Romans 1:16; Ephesians 6:17; 1 Thessalonians 1:5; 1 John 2:20-21;27).
- He has the power to guide the Devotee providentially (see Acts 8:26; 16:14).
- He has the power to produce "fruit" in the Devotee's life (see Galatians 5:22-23).
- He provides powerful spiritual gifts to advance the gospel in equipping the church (see 1 Corinthians 12:4-11) and building up the church (see Romans 12:3-8; 1 Corinthians 12:7-30; Ephesians 4:11-12; 1 Peter 4:10).

The Holy Spirit is dynamite, and you must believe and know that you *will* receive power.

Wait for it.

Trust in it.

You can't do it by yourself!

This is what I wish Leo had learned. I wish he had waited and learned to trust in Jesus—to leap into his loving arms and submit to his power; to experience that special thing that happens when Jesus catches us at just the right time.

He *will* catch you, so leap!

You can trust him, so hold on and enjoy the ride.

Trust me . . . it's a sacred trust.

CHAPTER 3

SEEING: LOVE AT FIRST SIGHT

And when he had said these things, as they were looking on,
he was lifted up, and a cloud took him out of their sight.
— *Acts 1:9*

HE WAS SEEN in the rust on top of Marcy Marksberry's corn silo.

He was seen in a cloud formation above Egypt.

People saw him in a shadow on a column in the school chapel of the Ursuline Academy in New Orleans.

Erica Scheldt saw him on the back of a dead stingray on Sullivan's Island, South Carolina.

He was sighted by a painter in the plaster on the wall behind a stereo in a house in Eldroth, North Yorkshire.

He was spotted on the floorboards of the Old Swan Inn in Paisley, Renfrewshire.

He was "clearly" seen in a clump of bird poo on the windshield of Jim Lawry's car.[4]

He was even seen on a dog's rear end.[5]

And Linda Lowe's life changed when she saw him on the grilled cheese sandwich her boyfriend prepared for her.[6]

Pareidolia is a psychological phenomenon where a seemingly insignificant image or sound is perceived as significant, so it should come as no surprise to anyone that many pareidolias involve seeing Jesus, because nothing is more significant than seeing Jesus.

Seeing Jesus changes your perspective forever.

Ask Mary, Joseph, and Simeon. They all marveled when they saw Jesus as a child in the temple (see Luke 2:33-34).

Ask that demon-possessed man in Capernaum—and those who saw his deliverance. They saw Jesus and were amazed (see Luke 4:36).

Ask the leper. He saw Jesus and immediately fell on his face before him, only to lift his eyes to see complete healing (see Luke 5:12).

Ask the multitudes. They saw Jesus and were delivered and healed (see Luke 6:18-19).

Ask the sinful woman. She saw Jesus in the Pharisee's house, worshipped him, and found salvation and peace (see Luke 7:50).

Ask the Gerasene demoniac. He saw Jesus and was released from the captivity of a demon named Legion (see Luke 8:26-39).

Ask the five thousand people. They saw Jesus when they

were hungry. He fed them with five loaves of bread and two fish, and they left full (see Luke 9:10-17).

Ask Peter, James, and John. They saw Jesus transfigured, and they were changed forever (see Luke 9:28-36).

Ask the ten lepers. They saw Jesus from a distance, and healing came to them (see Luke 17:11-19).

Ask the blind beggar. He couldn't see Jesus, but Jesus saw him and healed him—and both he and "all the people" suddenly saw Jesus (see Luke 18:35-43).

Ask Zacchaeus. He climbed a tree hoping to see Jesus and ended up experiencing what it's like to "*Eat with Saviors*" (see Luke 19:1-10).

Ask the Roman centurion. He saw Jesus die and was compelled to praise God and proclaim Christ's innocence (see Luke 23:47).

Ask the disciples. They saw Jesus after his resurrection and were filled with joy and amazement (see Luke 24:41).

Ask the apostles. They saw Jesus ascend into heaven and were so stunned by the sight that God had to send two angels to remind them to get back to work (Acts 1:11).

Seeing Jesus changes your perspective forever.

Ask *me*. I saw Jesus and couldn't get close to him quickly enough.

I've never expressed my testimony in writing before, but this feels like the perfect time.

I could tell you about living on the streets from a very young age. I could tell you about having to steal food daily in order to survive. I could tell you about joining a gang at the age of thirteen. I could tell you about being in and out of juvenile centers and several jails from the ages of fifteen to twenty-two. I could tell you about being addicted to various drugs and alcohol. I could tell you about fathering three kids before finally meeting the right woman and settling down. I could tell you about waking up early one morning in my own vomit, crying out to the Lord from my lowest point, and seeing a bright light in my dark spiritual cell at the moment he rescued me.

I could tell you about all of that, and you'd probably cry and think my testimony was incredibly powerful. But it wouldn't be true because I haven't done any of those things.

My testimony is pretty boring.

I'm a preacher's kid who was raised in a Christian home by two loving parents who were married twenty-eight years before my dad died. I went to church every Sunday morning and Sunday night, and most Wednesday nights for midweek Bible study. I was a pretty good kid who rarely got into any kind of trouble, but who was paddled one time in junior high for knocking on a classroom door during lunchtime. I've never smoked . . . anything! I didn't taste alcohol until college and then only had a few sips before I fell to my knees and repented for "falling away." Both my wife and I were virgins when we were married. We pay our taxes on time. I've only been ticketed for speeding twice, and I feel guilty walking past trash on the ground without picking it up and throwing it in the nearest trash receptacle.

Don't get me wrong! I'm far from perfect. Exhibit A: I

own a cat, I regularly speed, and I don't always skip that Mumford and Sons' song where they say the F-word about a dozen times, because I really like the tune.

Seriously, we're all sinners. I sin. Just like you. And sometimes I'm sure I sin with more flare than you could ever dream up. But still, my testimony is not dramatic, carnal, or full of the kind of stuff that would make an arena full of young Christians hold their breath, gasp in shock, weep, and flock to the altar because I showed them how close to hell (a direct reference to that hot place down below) an individual can get and still be forgiven by Jesus . . . and I don't think it has to be any of those things in order to be powerful.

I saw Jesus early and often in my home when I was a child.

I saw Jesus in the stories my mom and dad told me from the Bible.

I saw Jesus in the prayers my mom and dad offered up in our home and over me and my siblings.

I saw Jesus in the way my mom and dad loved each other.

I saw Jesus in the way my mom and dad loved me and my siblings.

I saw Jesus in the way my mom and dad served people.

I saw Jesus in the way my mom and dad worshipped.

I saw Jesus in the way my parents lived and, at just the right time—after a clearer understanding of my sin (at nine years old I got caught stealing gum from the local 7-Eleven) and my need for forgiveness (I knew enough of the Bible at that point in my life to figure you go to hell if you steal gum from the local 7-Eleven and never confess it)—I gave my life to Jesus, and I've never been the same since.

Seeing Jesus changes your perspective forever, and for me, truly seeing Jesus for the first time was love at first sight.

LOVE AT FIRST SIGHT

Do you believe in love at first sight? When it comes to romantic relationships, I'm not sure if I do. I've heard people I respect say they fell in love with their significant other at first sight, but I'm just not sure how that happens.

Lust at first sight . . . sure!

Like at first sight . . . I'll give you that.

Loathe at first sight . . . definitely!

My wife, Rhonda, loathed me the first time she saw me. I was an eighteen-year-old jerk who introduced myself to my future wife by ushering her off the college volleyball court so "just the guys could play." At that time, my arrogance and belief that I actually was one of the stars of the movie *Top Gun* blinded me to many things, such as the fact that she was a better volleyball player than any guy in the room . . . including me.

She left the court but refused to leave the gym, and she sat there scowling at me for the next hour. She'll tell you now she sat there resolving never to date a guy like me.

Thankfully, and by the grace of God, she forgave me enough to go out with me a couple of months later—and the rest is history—but it wasn't love at first sight.

But my relationship with Jesus was love at first sight . . . and I want the same for you.

In the movie *Avatar*, paraplegic marine Jake Sully joins a mission to a distant world called Pandora. On this planet he encounters the humanoids who live on that planet: the Na'vi. Over time he bonds with the Na'vi and falls in love with the beautiful, and very tall, and very blue, Neytiri. I won't spoil the movie for you by revealing any other major plot points, but I will tell you that, as Jake and Neytiri's relationship develops, we learn that the Na'vi have a unique way of saying, "I love you." They say, "I see you."

As you begin this relationship with Jesus, I want you to fall deeply in love with him. I want you to see him.

See Him as Son

When you see Jesus, you are seeing the Son of God.

Gabriel foretold that Jesus is the Son of God: "He will be great and will be called the Son of the Most High" (Luke 1:32). This confused Mary, so she asked for more clarification: "How will this be, since I am a virgin?" (Luke 1:34).

Good question.

Gabriel then clarified it a bit more: "The Holy Spirit will come upon you, and the power of the Most High will overshadow you; therefore the child to be born will be called holy—the Son of God" (Luke 1:35).

Jesus' ministry began with God pronouncing it: "This is my beloved Son, with whom I am well pleased" (Matthew 3:17). The demons Jesus cast out affirmed it: "Now when the sun was setting, all those who had any who were sick with various diseases brought them to him, and he laid his hands on every one of them and healed them. And demons also came out of many, crying, 'You are the Son of God!'" (Luke 4:40-41). Peter confessed it. "You are the Christ, the Son of the living God" (Matthew 16:16). Upon Christ's death, the Roman centurion acknowledged it. "Truly this man was the Son of God!" (Mark 15:39). John saw it for himself, so he testified to the importance of it. "And we have *seen* and testify that the Father has sent his Son to be the Savior of the world. Whoever confesses that Jesus is the Son of God, God abides in him, and he in God" (1 John 4:14-15, emphasis added).

You may have recently confessed it: "I believe that Jesus is the Christ, the Son of the living God, and my Lord and Savior."

But do you know what it means to see Jesus as the Son of God?

All of the first converts to Christianity were Jewish, and they were raised to regard themselves, corporately, as the "sons" of God. Of the Israelites the Lord said, "Then you shall say to Pharaoh, 'Thus says the LORD, Israel is my first-born son, and I say to you, "Let my son go that he may serve me"'" (Exodus 4:22-23). Because of this special relationship, the Jews had the blessing of experiencing the love, protection, comfort, and discipline children should expect from a loving father. The pagans also had familiarity with the name "son of god" because it was common for Egyptian, Babylonian, Canaanite, and Roman rulers to be called "son of god."[7]

When we confess that Jesus is the "Son of God," we are confessing that we see Jesus as being of the same substance as the Father (see Philippians 2:6), as having shared ownership of God's "house" (Luke 2:49), as having unity with the Father (see John 10:30), as acting in concert with the Father (see Mark 2:7-11), as being obedient to the Father (see Luke 22:42), as having a legal claim to the resources of the Father (see Malachi 1:6), as having equal authority with the Father (see John 3:35), as sharing in the Father's right to bring life and to judge (see John 5:21-24), as having absolute sovereignty in revealing the Father (see Matthew 11:25-27), as one who "enjoys intimacy and union with the Father (God), and also as one who reveals true knowledge of the Father (God)", and as the "divine Son who comes from God and who, through his eschatological person, makes God's fatherly presence available to all."[8]

Seeing Jesus as the Son of God, and confessing that truth, is ultimately a statement on his origin (we are saying he came from God—see John 13:3), it's a statement on his power (he's our only way to God—see John 14:6), and it's a statement on his nature ("Whoever has seen [Jesus] has seen the Father"—John 14:9).

See Him as Savior

It's also important, as you begin your relationship with Jesus, that you see him as your Savior. As Brennan Manning so clearly articulates in his book *The Furious Longing of God*, "The gospel is absurd and the life of Jesus is meaningless unless we believe that He lived, died, and rose again with but one purpose in mind: to make brand-new creations."[9]

Jesus died to save you and me from our sins and to make us new creations.

Do you know that you are a new creation? Do you see yourself as new? As changed?

When you look in the mirror from now on, I want you to see yourself as a new person in Christ.

He saved you in every way possible. What does that mean?

I love the apostle Paul's teaching on what it means to be saved.

For the love of Christ controls us, because we have concluded this: that one has died for all, therefore all have died; and he died for all, that those who live might no longer live for themselves but for him who for their sake died and was raised.

From now on, therefore, we regard no one according to the flesh. Even though we once regarded Christ according to the flesh, we regard him thus no longer. Therefore, if anyone is in Christ, he is a new creation. The old has passed away; behold, the new has come. All this is from God, who through Christ reconciled us to himself and gave us the ministry of reconciliation; that is, in Christ God was reconciling the world to himself, not counting their trespasses against them, and entrusting to us the message of reconciliation.

Therefore, we are ambassadors for Christ, God
making his appeal through us. We implore you on
behalf of Christ, be reconciled to God. For our sake
he made him to be sin who knew no sin, so that in
him we might become the righteousness of God.
(2 Corinthians 5:14-21)

Let's unpack this passage.

HE SAVED US FROM PUNISHMENT

Jesus died on a cross so that we could avoid being eternally
punished for our sins.

God is just, and because he's just, he has to punish sin.
The fact that he does what he says he's going to do and isn't
constantly changing the rules gives us security. Do you know
how unstable we'd be in our relationship with Jesus if God
were always changing the rules?

"Today, I've decided to allow murder."—God

"Well, that didn't work, so now murder is a sin again, but
lying is not."—God

"Oops . . . I lied! Lying is a sin again, but we're going
to see what happens if adultery is permitted for the next
week."—God

"That 'hell' thing . . . yeah, after consulting with Rob Bell
(or doing a Gallup survey), I decided that was a really bad
idea, so I snuffed it out yesterday."—God

This instability would be chaos.

If we lived in a world where we could not count on God

to do anything he said he was going to do, we would be doomed to live lives in constant chaos. But our lives in Christ are not chaotic because God has clearly identified the boundaries. Knowing the lines between right and wrong provides clear direction home through this dark and confusing world.

So, since God is just, he had to punish someone.

Under the Old Covenant (also known as the Law), God's people could only find forgiveness for their sins through the shedding of an animal's blood. "Indeed, under the law almost everything is purified with blood, and without the shedding of blood there is no forgiveness of sins" (Hebrews 9:22).

And the sacrifice had to be the best we could offer. It had to be perfect. And Jesus was.

Jesus was the best God had to offer, so God offered him as a sacrifice for our sins. "For our sake *he made him* to be sin *who knew no sin*, so that in him we might become the righteousness of God" (2 Corinthians 5:21, emphasis added).

Under the New Covenant (also known as grace), God decided to offer Jesus as a once-and-for-all, perfect sacrifice so we could find forgiveness for our sins.

Let me make an important point here. Since we are all sinners (see Romans 3:23) and as such are deserving of wrath (see Ephesians 2:3), we will encounter the wrath of God either at Calvary or on Judgment Day. If we give our lives to Christ and embrace the grace of God through the sacrifice of Jesus on the cross at Calvary, then—at the point when the wrath of God was poured out on Jesus (see Isaiah 53:6) in an act of divine justice on the cross over two thousand years ago—we are saved. But if we reject Jesus, then we will encounter the wrath of God, unprotected by the blood of Jesus, on the Day of Judgment.

Yes, Jesus saved us from punishment, but he also saved us for something else.

HE SAVED US FOR A NEW PURPOSE

I find it humorous that the apostles stood there looking into the sky as Jesus left (Acts 1:11); they should have known better.

Like a football team who just heard a rousing speech from their coach and received a winning game plan but are standing inside the locker room while the game commences outside, these apostles really dropped the ball.

Had Jesus not been perfectly clear? "All authority in heaven and on earth has been given to me. Go therefore and make disciples of all nations, baptizing them in the name of the Father and of the Son and of the Holy Spirit, teaching them to observe all that I have commanded you. And behold, I am with you always, to the end of the age" (Matthew 28:18-20).

They had a mission, a purpose for living, but they were standing there wasting time.

You have a mission, a purpose for living. "For we are his workmanship, created in Christ Jesus for good works, which God prepared beforehand, that we should walk in them" (Ephesians 2:10).

You've now seen Jesus, but don't stand there just staring at him. During this time of waiting on the Lord, begin to turn your attention to the people around you. Start seeing people.

See their hurts. See their confusion. See their desperation for hope. Start seeing people through the eyes of Christ because he wants them to see him as Savior too, which is why he sent the angels to remind the apostles, "This Jesus, who was taken up from you into heaven, will come in the same way as you saw him go into heaven" (Acts 1:11).

Jesus lived for us.

Jesus died for us.

Jesus rose again from the dead for us.

Jesus is coming again for us, and "every eye will see him" (Revelation 1:7).

At that moment, everyone will see Jesus, and for those who have given their lives to him, it will be love at first sight.

I loved Jesus the first time I saw him, but that wasn't the "love at first sight" I've been talking about in this chapter. I've been talking about the first time Jesus saw us. The first time Jesus saw you and me, it was love at first sight, and love at second sight, and love at third sight, and love at one hundred and third sight, and love at three hundred and forty-five thousandth sight, and love at eternal sight.

From the cross, Jesus was still loving us.

See him dying on that cross for your sins.

See him loving you with every cell in his body.

See him.

Look closely at his face. It's full of grace. It's full of forgiveness. It's full of love.

Look closely at his eyes. He's looking at you.

Look closely at his mouth, because he's trying to say

something to you. See it? He's saying it over and over again, and he's saying it to you.

Do you see what he's saying to you?

"I."

"See."

"You."

Seeing Jesus changes your perspective forever.

Ask my dad. He saw Jesus and resolved to spend the rest of his life helping others to see Jesus more clearly.

As I write this today, it's the twenty-fifth anniversary of my dad's sudden death. In the months before his death, my dad was struck with a serious eye problem that threatened to take his eyesight. Dad held a PhD in ancient history and human anthropology and was a preacher, an author, and a Bible college professor. Books were his passion, and the thought of losing his eyesight hit him hard. After his death, my mom told me that he was really scared to go blind and spent time praying and crying before the Lord. On August 8, 1988, Dad died of a heart attack while taking a nap. The time of death was about 1:44 p.m. At 1:45 p.m., he wasn't going blind anymore. At that very moment, he saw the Lord. I wonder what Dad's first conversation with Christ was like. They loved each other so much. I may be wrong, but I think it went something like this: "Roger, I see you!" To which Dad replied, "Jesus, I see you, too."

I hope you believe in love at first sight now, because I know I do.

CHAPTER 4

SPEAKING: TO TELL THE TRUTH

—————

But Peter, standing with the eleven, lifted up his voice and
addressed them.—Acts 2:14

As a professional communicator, I've learned it's important to know when to speak and when to be silent.

As a husband, not so much. In my twenty-three years of
marriage, I've become a professional at putting my foot in
my mouth.

I've learned that questions like, "Does this dress make
me look fat?" "Do you mind if my mom stays with us?" "Do
you think Scarlett Johansson is pretty?" and "Were you really
just checking your fantasy football scores while I was trying
to talk to you about how I feel about that situation?" are all
best answered with silence.

The daily news is currently dominated with stories of

people who are refusing to speak. A young man named Edward Snowden is hiding in Russia, refusing to speak about the American secrets he exposed. New York Yankee's third baseman Alex Rodriguez is refusing to answer questions about whether he used performance-enhancing drugs. Several IRS officials have recently been called before Congress on charges that they have treated some conservative groups unfairly, but they are all refusing to speak, exercising their Fifth-Amendment right to remain silent.

Silence is safe.

Silence protects.

Silence hides.

But as Christians, when it comes to the gospel, we have no right to remain silent, especially when the time is right.

TIMING IS EVERYTHING

Another thing I've learned as a professional communicator is that it's important not only to know what to say, but to know when to say it. It's important to say the right thing at the right time.

You won't be received well when you congratulate a woman at church on being pregnant when she's not pregnant. She will not be happy with the timing of that particular congratulatory observation.

It's going to get real uncomfortable when you congratulate your friend—in front of many friends—on finally getting the girl of his dreams to start dating him, only to find out that she ruthlessly dumped him on the phone minutes before you arrived at his house. He's not going to be happy with the timing of that bit of praise.

And—take it from me—it's not a good idea to announce to the church from the baptistery that the couple you are baptizing is getting married soon, when in fact he hasn't proposed yet. The couple being immersed, and the many members of her family who are surprised to hear that bit of news announced so cavalierly by a skinny preacher in waders, are not going to be happy with the timing of that pronouncement.

When it comes to speaking effectively, timing is everything.

I just left the hospice wing of one of our local hospitals. I went there to pray with a dear woman who is preparing to meet Jesus face-to-face and the loving family she's leaving behind. She's ready, and so is her family because they were able to say "good-bye" to their mother two days ago when she was still alert. There is peace in that place of grief because they said what they needed to say when they had a chance to say it. Timing is everything at the end of relationships, and timing is everything at the beginning of relationships.

After three months of dating my wife, Rhonda, it felt like the right time to speak the words that best described what I was feeling. I'm a pretty passionate guy, and I'd felt the full extent of these words since the first month of our relationship. However, I already understood Rhonda well enough to know that it would be best to wait for the right time.

My wife is a mysterious, beautiful, deep well. There's not

a shallow, superficial, or spontaneous cell in her body. She, unlike me, thinks before she speaks, and, even as an eighteen-year-old young woman, she wasn't about to speak those three words until she knew she meant them. I knew that, but my heart told me it was the right time to speak what I was feeling. So I spoke up at what I thought was the perfect time during one especially romantic evening.

"Rhonda, I love you."

To which she replied, "Thanks!"

Ouch! Epic fail!

Well, not really. Timing *is* everything. She eventually confessed her love for me at the real right time, and the rest is history.

Let's go back to those apostles staring at the sky. It was the right time for Peter to speak up, so he did. Jesus had ascended into heaven after giving the disciples both a specific promise and a purpose.

The promise: "You will receive power" (Acts 1:8).

The purpose: "You will be my witnesses in Jerusalem and in all Judea and Samaria, and to the end of the earth" (Acts 1:8).

A witness's job is, when he's called upon, to testify to what he has seen. In a court of law, witnesses who refuse to testify may be arrested and held in contempt of court. A witness's responsibility is to speak up at just the right time.

The apostles were being called upon to speak up, and it was definitely the right time.

The Holy Spirit had come down from heaven and given the apostles the supernatural ability to speak in all of the languages of all of the Jews who were gathered from all over the world for the Feast of Pentecost in Jerusalem. Everyone who heard them speaking in their own native tongue was amazed and curious about what was happening. They wanted answers, and Peter had them. So—with the full attention of the multitudes of lost people—Peter, knowing it was time to speak, stood up and shared the gospel.

Devotee, as a Christ-follower, you've also been called to be a witness for Christ and to share the gospel at just the right time. So in this period of waiting, as you begin your relationship with Jesus, begin asking God to give you wisdom as to when to speak up and when to be silent.

And, just to make sure I'm clear, I'm not saying that this is the right time for you to speak up for Jesus. I'm not saying it's the wrong time either. What I am saying is that timing is everything, and the time is coming, maybe sooner rather than later, when you will have the opportunity to speak up and share the gospel.

Some things aren't really considered true until spoken.

In our relationship with Jesus, it should come as no surprise, then, that he expects us to speak certain truths audibly.

If we are truly sorry for sinning against him, then we must confess it: "Therefore, confess your sins to one another and pray for one another, that you may be healed" (James 5:16). If we truly believe in him, then we must acknowledge it publicly: "So everyone who acknowledges me before men, I also will acknowledge before my Father who is in heaven, but whoever denies me before men, I also will deny before my Father who is in heaven" (Matthew 10:32-33). And, if we truly believe the gospel is true and the key to salvation for lost people, then true love demands that we must share it everywhere: "And the gospel must first be proclaimed to all nations" (Mark 13:10).

Let me stop here, before going any further, because I feel like I've gotten a little ahead of myself. Do you know what I mean when I say the word *gospel*?

SAY WHAT?

There are many words used among Christians that are what I call "insider" language.

Words like *stewardship, repentance, throne of grace, narthex, Communion, discipleship, traveling mercies, evangelism, blessed, doxology, benediction, prostrate (not prostate), potluck, born-again, redemption, justification, sanctification, ordained, propitiation, seeker-sensitive, washed in the blood, missional, sanctuary, Second Coming, fellowship, tithe, righteousness, hedge of protection, atonement, accountability, secular, cleansed, witness, guard her heart, backsliding, the Word, testimony, believer, saved, doctrine, relevant, devotion,* and *gospel,* to name a few.[10] Based on what we read in the New Testament, that last one, *gospel,* is pretty important:

- Jesus proclaimed it: "And he went throughout all Galilee, teaching in their synagogues and proclaiming the gospel of the kingdom and healing every disease and every affliction among the people" (Matthew 4:23).

- Losing your life for it will save you: "For whoever would save his life will lose it, but whoever loses his life for my sake and the gospel's will save it" (Mark 8:35).
- Jesus wants the world to hear it: "And he said to them, 'Go into all the world and proclaim the gospel to the whole creation'" (Mark 16:15).
- It holds the power to salvation: "For I am not ashamed of the gospel, for it is the power of God for salvation to everyone who believes, to the Jew first and also to the Greek" (Romans 1:16).
- The apostle Paul could not have been more committed to it: "Woe to me if I do not preach the gospel!" (1 Corinthians 9:16).
- It comes from God: "For I would have you know, brothers, that the gospel that was preached by me is not man's gospel" (Galatians 1:11).
- It should be the standard for our lives: "Only let your manner of life be worthy of the gospel of Christ" (Philippians 1:27).
- It saves us: "Now I would remind you, brothers, of the gospel I preached to you, which you received, in which you stand, and by which you are being saved, if you hold fast to the word I preached to you— unless you believed in vain" (1 Corinthians 15:1-2).
- And it's the most important thing ever: "For I delivered to you as of *first importance* what I also received" (1 Corinthians 15:3, emphasis added).

That last passage deserves further attention. Ancient Christian documents reveal that the *kerygma*, or "the preaching of the gospel," in the early church would often encompass only 1 Corinthians 15:3-8 because it's one of the clearest and most concise presentations of the gospel. They referred to the following verses as the "center" of the Bible (that is, the entire message of the Bible in six verses):

For I delivered to you as of first importance what I also received: that Christ died for our sins in accordance with the Scriptures, that he was buried, that he was raised on the third day in accordance with the Scriptures, and that he appeared to Cephas, then to the twelve. Then he appeared to more than five hundred brothers at one time, most of whom are still alive, though some have fallen asleep. Then he appeared to James, then to all the apostles. Last of all, as to one untimely born, he appeared also to me. (1 Corinthians 15:3-8)

I want you to continue to spend the next forty days waiting on the Lord—faithfully, patiently, and silently expecting the Lord to guide you toward the next steps you are to take in your relationship with him. And when God makes it evident to you that it's time for you to speak up and share the gospel, this is the message you must deliver. Jesus . . .

Died for our sins.

Was buried.

Was raised from the dead on the third day.

And appeared to more than five hundred people after his resurrection, including the apostle Paul.

This is the gospel we must speak, when the time is right.

THE TRUTH HURTS

Moms sometimes lie.

At least my mom did each time she declared, "Sticks and stones may break my bones, but words will never hurt me," because sometimes words *really* hurt.

And sometimes that's okay. Sometimes we need words to hurt so that they can heal.

"We found termites."

"We found a major leak in the basement."

"We found cancer."

"If you don't start eating healthy and lose some weight, you're going to die."

"We need some marriage counseling."

"Your husband is not coming back, and you need to let go and move on."

"You hurt me."

"Your kids need you."

"Arron, you're flaky and sometimes you don't follow through with what you say you're going to do."

"Let all the house of Israel therefore know for certain that God has made him both Lord and Christ, this Jesus whom you crucified" (Acts 2:36).

The truth hurts, and this was the truth.

The time was right, and so was Peter as he held up a verbal

mirror before the crowd of Jewish people and let them see Jesus on the cross and let them realize that they had crucified him.

His words hurt.

Luke records, "Now when they heard this they were cut to the heart" (Acts 2:37). As Dietrich Bonhoeffer wrote, "Nothing can be more cruel than the tenderness that consigns another to his sin. Nothing can be more compassionate than the severe rebuke that calls a brother back from the path of sin."[11]

The truth Peter stood up and spoke was a severe rebuke, but it was not cruel. Cruel would have been allowing these people to pack up and head back to their villages and towns without the awareness that they had witnessed to and participated in the execution of the Messiah, whose coming they both longed for and needed. With just two words they spoke up and delivered the Word to Pontius Pilate for execution. "Crucify him" (Mark 15:13,14).

The truth Peter stood up and spoke was compassionate because he was telling lost travelers how to get home. Convicted of their mistake, the people asked, "Brothers, what shall we do?" (Acts 2:37).

Throughout the Bible, God asks people to act on their convictions.

"Noah, you believe me? Build an ark" (see Genesis 6:14).

"Abraham, you believe me? Put Isaac on the altar" (see Genesis 22:2).

"Moses, you believe me? Go and speak to Pharaoh" (see Exodus 3:10).

"Joshua, you believe me? Walk around Jericho" (see Joshua 6:2-7).

"Naaman, you believe me? Go and dip yourself in the Jordan River seven times" (see 2 Kings 5:10).

"Rich young ruler, you believe me? Leave everything you have and follow me" (see Luke 18:22).

"Jewish people gathered for the Feast of Pentecost, you believe me? 'Repent and be baptized every one of you in the name of Jesus Christ for the forgiveness of your sins, and you will receive the gift of the Holy Spirit'(Acts 2:38)."

THE TRUTH HEALS

In the book of Acts we see a pattern in the responses of those who receive the truth of the gospel of Jesus Christ. Those lost people who receive the gospel are either called upon, or feel personally compelled, to take specific actions because of their newfound faith in Christ.

We find healing through our faith in Christ.

Now, Luke doesn't specifically cite "faith" on behalf of these Jewish converts in this account, but it's logically inferred based on their response to Peter's message, "Brothers, what shall we do?" (Acts 2:37). They heard the gospel through Peter, believed what they were hearing, felt convicted of their sin of rejecting the Messiah, and were worried about being lost forever because of their sin—so they cried out for salvation.

Like the person who is told he has a terrible form of cancer that will take his life unless he follows the right course of action, these people heard they were in big trouble, and they wanted to know what they needed to do to be saved. They asked the questions because they had faith that God had the power to save them. I find that very interesting. When you are in trouble, whom do you ask for help? You have faith in whomever you ask.

I can't imagine how terrifying it feels to find oneself in trouble but to have no one to ask for help.

Imagine being lost in a desert and no one is looking for you.

Imagine having a cancer diagnosis and you find out there are no more oncologists on the face of the planet.

Imagine having not a penny to your name and you're surrounded by paupers.

Imagine finding yourself locked in a dark prison and you find out there are no guards and there is no warden.

This must be what it's like for people who have no faith in anyone but themselves. This must be what it was like for the countless people in Jerusalem on the Day of Pentecost who rejected the gospel and went home still wishing for the advent of the Messiah who would hear their cries and heal them.

Peter testified to what he had witnessed, and about three thousand people believed what he was saying, received it as the gospel about Jesus Christ, and found eternal healing: "And with many other words he bore witness and continued to exhort them, saying, 'Save yourselves from this crooked generation.' So those who received his word were baptized, and there were added that day about three thousand souls" (Acts 2:40-41).

They were saved that day.

Healed.

When they received the gospel.

Through faith in Christ.

And so were you when you put your faith in Christ, but you were also healed when you repented of your sins.

We find healing through the repenting of our sins.

The Bible is clear: God wants us to repent. "The times of ignorance God overlooked, but now he commands all people everywhere to repent" (Acts 17:30).

The Jews at the Feast of Pentecost who believed the gospel were told to do it: "And Peter said to them, 'Repent and be baptized every one of you in the name of Jesus Christ for the forgiveness of your sins, and you will receive the gift of the Holy Spirit'" (Acts 2:38). The people in Solomon's Portico, who witnessed and were amazed at the healing of the lame beggar, were told to do it: "Repent therefore, and turn back, that your sins may be blotted out" (Acts 3:19).

You did it, but still, let me define it for you: Repentance is when we stop following sin and start following God.

Repentance was on that list of "insider" words used by Christians within the confines of the church, but not used much elsewhere. Problem is, in my opinion, I don't see that we "insiders" talk about it much or do it enough inside our confines. I may be wrong. If so, I'll repent, but think about it: When was the last time you saw or heard anyone repent of anything at a gathering of your church or small group? When was the last time you heard a sermon on repentance?

I remember the last time I spoke on repentance. It was last fall. I was finishing a message on repentance when I felt compelled by the Holy Spirit to repent of something, right there in front of people.

Palms sweating.

Knees shaking.

Canyon opening in the pit of my stomach.

"Job Security" light flashing in the back of my mind.

Knowing it was the right time.

I spoke up and confessed to the church that I sometimes struggle with lust. I told them that I'm not looking at porn, purposely flirting with other women, or cheating on my wife, but I struggle with looking away when I see a beautiful woman in person or online.

Then I repented of that sin.

Based on the reactions I received, you would have thought that I practiced spontaneous human combustion and two-thirds of the church consisted of pyromaniacs and the other third worked for Smokey Bear.

When I finished, men came to me, in tears, thanking me for modeling repentance and for making our church a "safe place" to be a sinner. Wives thanked me for being "a good example" for their husbands, and others asked me to pray for their husbands who struggle with the same thing. Others, though, seemed completely uncomfortable with my transparency, with a few reprimanding me for "allowing my emotions to get the best of me."

It was one of the hardest things I've ever done in ministry, and, as I look back on it now, I'm even more convinced that it had little to do with emotions and everything to do with healing. Mine and others'. Repentance needed to be experienced for healing to occur in my life, and now I realize it had to be done for healing to be released in the lives of some of the men and women in our church.

You repented.

Keep repenting. Repentance is healing, and it's always the right time for healing.

We also find healing through baptism.

How can something so clear become so muddied?

Jesus did it: "Then Jesus came from Galilee to the Jordan to John, to be baptized by him. John would have prevented him, saying, 'I need to be baptized by you, and do you come to me?' But Jesus answered him, 'Let it be so now, for thus it is fitting for us to fulfill all righteousness.' Then he consented. And when Jesus was baptized, immediately he went up from the water, and behold, the heavens were opened to him, and he saw the Spirit of God descending like a dove and coming to rest on him; and behold, a voice from heaven said, 'This is my beloved Son, with whom I am well pleased'" (Matthew 3:13-17).

He commanded his disciples to do it: "Go therefore and make disciples of all nations, baptizing them in the name of the Father and of the Son and of the Holy Spirit, teaching them to observe all that I have commanded you. And behold, I am with you always, to the end of the age" (Matthew 28:19-20).

And as we just saw, the people who received the gospel and put their faith in Christ did it on the Day of Pentecost. "So those who received his word were baptized, and there were added that day about three thousand souls" (Acts 2:41).

Throughout the book of Acts, people who received the gospel and put their faith in Christ did it:

But when they believed Philip as he preached good news about the kingdom of God and the name of Jesus Christ, they were baptized, both men and women. (Acts 8:12)

Even Simon himself believed, and after being baptized he continued with Philip. And seeing signs and great miracles performed, he was amazed. (Acts 8:13)

And as they were going along the road they came to some water, and the eunuch said, "See, here is water! What prevents me from being baptized?" And he commanded the chariot to stop, and they both went down into the water, Philip and the eunuch, and he baptized him. (Acts 8:36,38)

And immediately something like scales fell from his eyes, and he regained his sight. Then he rose and was baptized. (Acts 9:18)

And he commanded them to be baptized in the
name of Jesus Christ. (Acts 10:48)

And after she was baptized, and her household as
well, she urged us, saying, "If you have judged me
to be faithful to the Lord, come to my house and
stay." And she prevailed upon us. (Acts 16:15)

And he took them the same hour of the night and
washed their wounds; and he was baptized at
once, he and all his family. (Acts 16:33)

Crispus, the ruler of the synagogue, believed
in the Lord, together with his entire household.
And many of the Corinthians hearing Paul
believed and were baptized. (Acts 18:8)

On hearing this, they were baptized in the
name of the Lord Jesus. (Acts 19:5)

And now why do you wait? Rise and be baptized and wash
away your sins, calling on his name. (Acts 22:16)

The apostles wrote about it:

Do you not know that all of us who have been baptized into Christ Jesus were baptized into his death? We were buried therefore with him by baptism into death, in order that, just as Christ was raised from the dead by the glory of the Father, we too might walk in newness of life.

For if we have been united with him in a death like his, we shall certainly be united with him in a resurrection like his. (Romans 6:3-5)

In him also you were circumcised with a circumcision made without hands, by putting off the body of the flesh, by the circumcision of Christ, having been buried with him in baptism, in which you were also raised with him through faith in the powerful working of God, who raised him from the dead. (Colossians 2:11-12)

For as many of you as were baptized into Christ have put on Christ. (Galatians 3:27)

Baptism, which corresponds to this, now saves you, not as a removal of dirt from the body but as an appeal to God for a good conscience, through the resurrection of Jesus Christ. (1 Peter 3:21)

People do it at Journey. We've baptized 185 people so far this year.

You just did it . . . didn't you? If you haven't been baptized yet, here are some important things to consider.

The Greek word for baptism is *baptizo*, which means "to dip, submerge, to plunge, immerse."[12] It's the same word that was used for dyeing a piece of fabric. At the church where I serve, we baptize people by immersing them in water.

Now, I want to be clear at this point: I don't believe baptism—getting dunked under water—by itself saves you, but I believe the Bible teaches that baptism, when it is preceded by belief, repentance, and confession, is an essential part of the salvation process.

Some people say that you don't need to be baptized as a part of the salvation process because we are not saved by works. I agree, we are not saved by works—"For by grace you have been saved through faith. And this is not from your own doing; it is the gift of God, not a result of works, so that no one may boast" (Ephesians 2:8-9). If you get baptized without putting your faith in Jesus, you have not experienced a new beginning—you have just gotten wet.

But if you have been baptized because you put your faith in Jesus, you have not only experienced a new beginning—you have also experienced healing.

• • •

Today, at my office, I met with a woman who was released from jail three years ago. She'd been serving time for drug crimes. She's now sober. She's clean. She's going to a local community college to get a degree in psychology. She has a job. She's been faithfully attending our church for the past year. She has come far but still feels broken. She described herself to me as "broken pieces of glass held together with a pretty bow—everything looks good on the outside, but at any moment could fall apart."

Hearing her talk of her brokenness and need for healing, I knew the time was right, so I spoke up and asked her if she had a relationship with Jesus. She started to cry. Her next words revealed how unlovable she felt: "How could Jesus love me after all I've done?"

Knowing I had no right to remain silent, I spoke up again. My next words revealed how much Jesus loved her.

No, in all these things we are more than conquerors through him who loved us. For I am sure that neither death nor life, nor angels nor rulers, nor things present nor things to come, nor powers, nor height nor depth, nor anything else in all creation, will be able to separate us from the love of God in Christ Jesus our Lord. (Romans 8:37-39)

I shared the gospel and was powerfully reminded, as she received the gospel and asked to be baptized, the Truth still heals.

CHAPTER 5

LEARNING: "A MIND IS A TERRIBLE THING TO WASTE"

And they devoted themselves to the apostles'
teaching.—Acts 2:42

IN 1971 a philanthropic group called the United Negro College Fund (UNCF) ran a nationwide campaign to enable African-American young people to go to college. Their slogan became one the most popular slogans in the history of advertising: "A mind is a terrible thing to waste." In the last forty years, this campaign has raised over $1 billion and helped to send over 350,000 African-American young people through college.[13]

I agree, a mind is a terrible thing to waste. Do you know how extraordinary your mind is?

The human brain weighs about 3 pounds.

The brain is made up of about 75 percent water.

Your brain consists of about 100 billion neurons.

There are anywhere from 1,000 to 10,000 synapses for each neuron.

There are no pain receptors in the brain, so the brain can feel no pain.

There are 100,000 miles of blood vessels in the brain.

Information can be processed as slowly as 0.5 meters per second or as fast as 120 meters per second (about 268 miles per hour).

While awake, your brain generates between 10 and 23 watts of power—or enough energy to power a lightbulb.

You can't tickle yourself because your brain distinguishes between unexpected external touch and your own touch.

Every time you recall a memory or have a new thought, you are creating a new connection in your brain.[14]

Our brains are incredible vessels God created to be filled with life-changing and life-transforming information like baseball statistics, nursery rhymes, recipes, social security numbers, the alphabet song, the Pledge of Allegiance, the ingredients to a McDonald's Big Mac, "The Preamble" song from *Schoolhouse Rock!*, "It's a Small World After All," "My name is Inigo Montoya. You killed my father. Prepare to die," and the lyrics to the Charlie Daniels Band song "The Devil Went Down to Georgia."

What are we thinking? Literally!

So much with which we occupy our brains is the equivalent of filling the Holy Grail with gum balls.

A mind is a terrible thing to waste, so as you begin your relationship with Christ, I want you to seek to learn all you can about your groom, Jesus (see John 3:29). Why wouldn't you want to learn as much as you can about the One with whom you will be in a relationship for all eternity?

Those early conversations with a romantic interest are all about getting to know one another: When were you born? Where were you born? What are your hobbies? What is your family like? What activities were you involved with in high school? What do you want to do with your life? How many kids do you want to have? Where would you like to live in the future? Where would you like to travel? What are your dreams for the future? Who is your favorite college football team? The answers to these questions can make or break a relationship.

If you are interested in having a relationship with someone, then you will be interested in the facts of his or her life—not because you want to know *about* the person but because you want to know the person. Well, that's how it should be.

Do you want to know Jesus or merely know about him? You can know about him and not really know him, but you can't really know him and not know about him. And I'd propose that you can learn about him and not really love him, but you can't really love him and not want to learn about him.

Learning is loving.

Loving is learning.

When Rhonda and I were falling in love, we would talk for long stretches of time as we learned about each other. It was reckless. It was exciting. It was exhausting! Regularly, in those early days of our relationship, we would talk endlessly . . . learning about each other . . . falling in love . . . becoming more and more devoted to each other.

As you fall more and more in love with Jesus, you will naturally want to learn more about him. This is what the first Christ-followers experienced. "And they devoted themselves to the apostles' teaching" (Acts 2:42).

THE APOSTLES

In this book, I've referred several times to the men Jesus called to launch the church in Jerusalem and spread the gospel around the world as "apostles." However, I'm wondering, since we're talking about learning, if anyone has ever taught you what an apostle is. Well, let's learn.

First, let me teach you what a disciple is. A disciple is a student, so the disciples of Jesus were students of Jesus. They often called him "Rabbi," (Matthew 26:49; Mark 9:5; John 4:31) which is Jewish for "teacher." If you are a student of Jesus Christ, then you are a disciple of Jesus Christ. Which begs the question: Are you a good student of Jesus?

I wasn't the best student when I was growing up. For me, school was more of a social experience than an educational experience. Don't get me wrong. I studied, but only enough to maintain a solid B or C average. I could have gotten straight As, but I didn't always apply myself. I never set the curve. Looking back, I wasted a lot of opportunities to learn because I wasn't focused on learning. It wasn't until my sophomore year of college, after my dad's sudden death, that I started getting serious about learning, and then I couldn't get enough. I went on to earn a bachelor's degree in preaching, a bachelor's degree in theology, and a master's degree in church history and theology.

Now I love to learn. I can't get enough of Jesus, and I find myself wishing I hadn't waited so long to start learning.

Don't wait to learn about Jesus. Don't get a C in Christianity when you are capable of getting an A. Apply yourself. Set the curve.

Begin your relationship with Jesus with a devotion to learn as much as you can about the One who loved you as much as he could.

Second, let me define another important term, and the theme of this book, *discipleship*.

Okay, I just Googled the question, "What is discipleship?" and instantly gleaned a plethora of results that I found beautifully written and well intentioned but also somewhat unhelpful and unclear. Here are a few of my favorites:

Discipleship is the *diligent* and *intentional* teachings and *practices* that promote the life-long lifestyle of becoming ever more like Jesus and reproducing the Christ-life in others.[15] (The Assemblies of God)

Christian discipleship is the process by which disciples grow in the Lord Jesus Christ and are equipped by the Holy Spirit, who resides in our hearts, to overcome the pressures and trials of this present life and become more and more Christlike.[16] (Got Questions Ministries)

Discipleship is modeling and teaching Christians the precepts of the Bible–mainly prayer, doctrine, Christian living, and worship.[17] (Into Thy Word Ministries)

Yes, there are a lot of definitions for *discipleship*, and most of them are—like these definitions—perfectly fine. Others, though, are flavored with a legalism toxic to a healthy and loving relationship with Jesus. Like this definition I found:

What is discipleship? It is primarily obedience to the Savior. Discipleship includes many things. It is chastity. It is tithing. It is family home evening. It is keeping all the commandments.[18] (The Church of Jesus Christ of Latter-day Saints)

This definition of discipleship explains why there are two young men wearing white shirts, ties, dark pants, and name tags identifying themselves as "Elder so-and-so," riding their bikes somewhere in your town right now looking for doors upon which to knock. For members of the Church of Jesus Christ of Latter-day Saints (LDS), discipleship is about legalism not love, duty not devotion, and performance not passion for Jesus.

But this legalistic, duty-bound, and performance-based approach to discipleship is not limited to the official website of this aforementioned movement. You can also find hints of it scattered here and there in teachings on discipleship in mainstream evangelical Christianity.

In researching for this book, I stumbled upon an article in *Christianity Today* entitled "Eight Keys to Discipling New Christians." This article contains some helpful teaching on how to make disciples, but it also contains suggestions that I think place a little too much emphasis on duty and performance and not enough emphasis on heartfelt devotion to Jesus. Let me give you an example.

In a section entitled "Equip yourself," the author gives this instruction for preparing oneself for the act of discipleship:

> Go back and reread all of those verses you clung to
> when you were a new Christian. Memorize as much
> of Romans as you can. Look for natural openings to
> share God's Word, and use an easy-to-understand
> Bible translation. New believers inevitably have
> serious concerns about theological issues and
> always seem to get around to the 'Why do bad
> things happen to good people?' question. Study the
> Scriptures so that you are prepared to answer these
> questions when they are asked.[19]

So discipleship involves rereading "all of those verses you clung to when you were a new Christian," memorizing "as much of Romans as you can," securing and using "an easy-to-understand Bible translation," and being prepared to answer "Why do bad things happen to good people?" I don't know about you, but that would be enough to make me want to buy a bike, start calling myself "Elder Chambers," and spend the next two years tooling around Duluth, Minnesota, with my well-dressed buddy.

I'm not saying we shouldn't read and memorize Scripture, purchase a Bible we can understand, and consider some of life's hard questions as a part of discipleship. Of course we should do those things! This chapter is about learning. I'm just afraid, in our efforts to "do" discipleship, we sometimes forget the importance of "being" in a relationship with Jesus.

But I'm getting a little ahead of myself.

As you've seen, there are a lot of definitions for discipleship. Let me add one more. In my book on evangelism, *Eats with Sinners*, I define *evangelism* as "an intentional relationship through which someone is introduced to Jesus Christ." This book is a companion to that book, so—in light of the relational emphasis I teach regarding evangelism—in this book I'm offering this definition of discipleship:

An intentional relationship through which a Christian helps another Christian to fall more in love with Jesus.

When you love people and are devoted to them, you'll want to spend time with them, serve them, talk with them, submit to them, honor them, give generously to them, sacrifice for them, memorize books written by them to Christians in Rome, and learn about them.

All of this is love.

All of this is devotion.

All of this is discipleship . . . at least the kind of discipleship I'm promoting in this book and the kind of discipleship I see in the first Devotees to Christ.

In the New Testament, there are two primary usages of the term *apostle*. In one usage an apostle is someone who is sent out into the world on behalf of Jesus with an important message (see Acts 15:2,4,6,22-23; 16:4), and in another an apostle is someone who holds a position of special authority in the church (see Ephesians 4:11). All *apostles* (those who were sent out on behalf of Jesus) were *disciples* (students of Jesus), but not all *disciples* (students of Jesus) were *apostles* (sent out on behalf of Jesus) and not all *apostles* (sent out on behalf of Jesus) were *apostles* (special authority and office in the church). Understand?

The twelve apostles held unique positions as leaders who, with Christ as the "cornerstone," were considered as the "foundation" of the church now and in the New Jerusalem (see Ephesians 2:20; Revelation 21:14).

The twelve apostles held the most important office in the church: "And God has appointed in the church first apostles, second prophets, third teachers, then miracles, then gifts of healing, helping, administrating, and various kinds of tongues" (1 Corinthians 12:28).

The twelve apostles were also distinguished from the other apostles in the following ways:

- All of the apostles were called by Jesus to be apostles: "And when day came, he called his disciples and chose from them twelve, whom he named apostles" (Luke 6:13); "Paul, an apostle—not from men nor through man, but through Jesus Christ and God the Father" (Galatians 1:1).
- All of the apostles had personally seen Jesus after he rose from the dead. (The apostle Paul, even though he was called to be an apostle after the ascension of Jesus, was considered an apostle because he saw Jesus on the road to Damascus—see Acts 9:4-5; 1 Corinthians 9:1.): "And with great power the apostles were giving their testimony to the resurrection of the Lord Jesus, and great grace was upon them all" (Acts 4:33).
- All of the apostles had special authority: "I will give you the keys of the kingdom of heaven, and whatever you bind on earth shall be bound in heaven, and whatever you loose on earth shall be loosed in heaven" (Matthew 16:19).
- All of the apostles had the ability to do miracles: "And awe came upon every soul, and many wonders and signs were being done through the apostles" (Acts 2:43); "The signs of a true apostle were performed

among you with utmost patience, with signs and wonders and mighty works" (2 Corinthians 12:12).

- All of the apostles had the ability to lay their hands on other apostles and pass on the gift of the Holy Spirit and the ability to do miracles: "Then they laid their hands on them and they received the Holy Spirit. Now when Simon saw that the Spirit was given through the laying on of the apostles' hands, he offered them money" (Acts 8:17-18); "And when Paul had laid his hands on them, the Holy Spirit came on them, and they began speaking in tongues and prophesying" (Acts 19:6).[20]

Okay, so now that we've learned what an apostle is, we need to learn what they taught.

THE APOSTLES' TEACHING

As we read in Acts 2:42, the first Christ-followers were devoted to something called "the apostles' teaching." What is "the apostles' teaching"?

The Greek word for "teaching" in this verse is the word *didache*, which also means "doctrine." Through the years, both of these terms have been well defined and have come to represent two very important elements of the church at large.

The Didache, a document detailing the teachings of the twelve apostles, came into existence in the late first or early second century. The "apostles' teaching" of which we read in Acts 2:42 would certainly be represented in *The Didache*, but the "apostles' teaching" we're discussing is not this official document.

The *doctrine* that is so often referred to in church is the set of beliefs that any particular church, or the church at large, holds to, believes, and teaches. The "apostles' teaching" of which we read in Acts 2:42 would certainly contain key elements (hopefully) of any list of church doctrine you'd find on a flyer in the foyer of any evangelical church around the world, but the "apostles' teaching" of which I speak is not necessarily the same thing you may think of when you hear or read the word *doctrine*.

The "apostles' teaching" to which these first Christ-followers were devoted simply meant teachings from the apostles about Jesus—what they learned from him, what they experienced with him, and what he told them to teach. And the "apostles' teaching" most certainly honored Christ's commission in Matthew 28:

And Jesus came and said to them, "All authority in heaven and on earth has been given to me. Go therefore and make disciples of all nations, baptizing them in the name of the Father and of the Son and of the Holy Spirit, *teaching them to observe all that I have commanded you.* And behold, I am with you always, to the end of the age." (Matthew 28:18-20, emphasis added)

So if the "apostles' teaching" included the teaching of "all that [Jesus] . . . commanded," then we need to take a moment and look at some of what Jesus commanded while he was with the apostles. Any Devotee to Christ would do well to learn these commands and seek to obey them as he or she begins a relationship with Jesus.

THE COMMANDS OF JESUS

Jesus commands us to:

- Forgive (see Matthew 6:12).
- Be born again (see John 3:7).
- Abide in him (see John 15:4).
- Do good works (see Matthew 5:16).
- Do whatever it takes to avoid sin (see Matthew 5:29-30).
- Let our "yes" be "yes" and our "no" be "no" (see Matthew 5:34-37).
- Not seek revenge (see Matthew 5:38-39).
- Love our enemies (see Matthew 5:43-45).
- Give to the needy (see Matthew 6:2).
- Pray (see Matthew 6:5-7).
- Forgive others (see Matthew 6:14).
- Fast (see Matthew 6:16).
- Lay up treasures in heaven (see Matthew 6:19-20).
- Not worry (see Matthew 6:25-32,34).
- Seek his kingdom first (see Matthew 6:33).
- Not judge on matters that are God's to judge (see Matthew 7:1-2).
- Take care of the poor (see Matthew 25:34-36).

- Beware of false prophets (see Matthew 7:15).
- Observe the Lord's Supper in remembrance of him (see Luke 22:19-20).
- Show mercy to others (see Luke 6:36).
- Go to people all over the world, teach them these things, and baptize them in the name of the Father, Son, and Holy Spirit (see Matthew 28:19-20).
- Love people (see Matthew 22:39).
- Love God (see Matthew 22:37).

These are some of the things that the apostles taught and to which the first Christ-followers were devoted.

Devotee, live these.

Love these.

Learn these, because the United Negro College fund slogan is right. A mind is a terrible thing to waste.

CHAPTER 6

SHARING: ON POUNDCAKE-FILLED PURSES

———

And they devoted themselves to . . . fellowship.—Acts 2:42

W HEN YOU HEAR the word *fellowship*, what comes to mind?

Do you think about a financial grant given to a scholar so he or she can attend a university?

Do you think of four hobbits, a wizard, an elf, a dwarf, the son of Denethor, and a stud ranger on their way to destroy a ring in the fires of Mordor?

When I hear the word *fellowship*, I think about Mrs. Anderson.

Well, no . . . think about a potluck meal eaten after Sunday morning church services.

No, that's not quite accurate either. If I'm being honest, it's hard for me to hear the word *fellowship* and not think of pound cake. Why? I'm glad you asked.

The church I attended as a young man was famous for what we called fellowship dinners. A fellowship dinner was a potluck meal enjoyed by the entire congregation after the Sunday morning worship service, which was typically held in a room called the Fellowship Hall.

My memories of these glorious feasts are glutted with platters full of deviled eggs, piles of fresh fried chicken, steaming dishes of green bean casserole adorned with fried onions, bowls of fresh radishes, spiral-sliced ham, warm apple pie, and the image of Mrs. Anderson stuffing a pound cake into her purse.

I can't remember a fellowship dinner from my youth, at least as long as Mrs. Anderson was alive, when I didn't witness her fill up her plate, well past its rated limitations, and then—when she reached the dessert portion of the table—open up her large purse, insert an entire pound cake, and then immediately leave the building.

I'm not sure Mrs. Anderson understood fellowship.

Do you?

As you sit there by yourself, waiting on the Lord to guide you as you begin your relationship with him, I want you to realize that you are not alone, nor were you designed to be.

God created us for fellowship with him.

- In the Garden of Eden, God "walked" with Adam and Eve before they ate their way out of house and home: "And they heard the sound of the Lord God walking in the garden in the cool of the day" (Genesis 3:8).

- God created Eve for Adam because he wanted Adam to have fellowship with another person. God said, "It is not good that the man should be alone; I will make him a helper fit for him" (Genesis 2:18).
- God released the children of Israel from bondage to have fellowship with them: "I will make my dwelling among you, and my soul shall not abhor you. And I will walk among you and will be your God, and you shall be my people" (Leviticus 26:11-12).
- God wants to have fellowship with us through the Holy Spirit: "Whoever keeps his commandments abides in God, and God in him. And by this we know that he abides in us, by the Spirit whom he has given us" (1 John 3:24).
- He wants us to have fellowship with Christ: "God is faithful, by whom you were called into the fellowship of his Son, Jesus Christ our Lord" (1 Corinthians 1:9).
- God wants to have fellowship with anyone and everyone who will welcome him in: "Behold, I stand at the door and knock. If anyone hears my voice and opens the door, I will come in to him and eat with him, and he with me" (Revelation 3:20).

So what is fellowship? There are a lot of great definitions out there. Here's mine: "companions sharing life for their mutual benefit and the benefit of others."

God wants fellowship with us for our benefit (blessings; see John 1:14), for how that relationship will benefit him (worship; see John 4:23), and for how that relationship will benefit the world (faith; see John 17:20-21). To that end Jesus prayed, "I do not ask for these only, but also for those who will believe in me through their word, that they may all be one, just as you, Father, are in me, and I in you, that they also may be in us, so that the world may believe that you have sent me" (John 17:20-21).

Devotee, I need you to be on your guard in this area.

I need you.

You need me.

We need each other.

You need to be careful. Satan wants to isolate you so that you are easier to destroy. He's not an idiot, so he won't attack you when you're experiencing fellowship with brothers and sisters in Christ. No, he'll come to you when you're alone, like right now, and whisper lies in your ear.

"You can't trust them."

"They don't really like you."

"You don't need them.

"You deserve to be treated better than that."

"This is going to end up with you being hurt, so you might as well leave them now, before it all goes bad."

Yes, Satan is a liar, a thief, and a murderer; he is intent on destroying everything that bears the mark of the Maker (see John 10:10).

WE HAVE A COMMON ENEMY

I've been using his name, but I'm wondering if you even know who Satan is. I know you know his name, but do you know who he is?

Let's start with what we know about Satan.

In the Bible Satan (which means "adversary") is called by several other names, including "the devil" (1 John 3:8), "the father of lies" (John 8:44), "Lucifer" (Isaiah 14:12, KJV), and "the prince of the power of the air" (Ephesians 2:2).

We don't know what Satan looks like. Throughout the ages, Satan has been depicted in a variety of ways—all evil and scary.

What do you picture when you read that name—*Satan*?

Pitchfork? Horns? Red skin? Long, forked tail? Bat wings?

Speaking of bat wings, C. S. Lewis has a deeply profound theory for why the Devil and demons have often been depicted by artists as having bats' wings and angels as having birds' wings: "not because anyone holds that moral deterioration would be likely to turn feathers into membranes, but because most men like birds better than bats."[21]

Nothing in the biblical description of Satan suggests he holds a pitchfork or has horns, red skin, a long, forked tail, or bat wings. Paul gives a more accurate—and I believe a scarier—picture of how Satan appears: "And no wonder, for even Satan disguises himself as an angel of light" (2 Corinthians 11:14).

So Satan looks like a sweet little shining cherub. Next Halloween, I dare you to dress like a cherub angel and try to convince people you're really Satan. That should be fun!

But that's why Satan is so deadly. Like the serial killer who lives next door, mows his yard when it needs to be mowed, pays his taxes on time, shovels your snow periodically, waves when he sees you pulling into your driveway, sits on the local school board, and shops at Walmart, Satan doesn't look like we'd expect him to look. We can be easily caught off guard and devoured, leaving our loved ones uttering in disbelief before a local news crew, "He seemed like such a nice guy." Cut yourself some slack—you don't expect a sweet little shining cherub to want to devour you. But that's what he does and who he is, so cut him no slack.

WHO IS THE DEVIL?

Before I go any further, I need to ask: Do you believe in the Devil? According to researcher George Barna, forty percent of Christians do not believe that the Devil is a living being, but rather that he is only a "symbol of evil."[22] I'm more terrified by this statistic than I am of the Devil. How can you fight against someone you don't believe exists? Why would you fight against someone you don't believe exists? How can a Christ-follower deny the existence of the being Christ died on a cross to defeat?

Maybe I should pause here and clarify what I mean by "the Devil," using C. S. Lewis's explanation for what he meant by "the Devil":

> If by "the Devil" you mean a power opposite to God and, like God, self-existent from all eternity, the answer is certainly No. There is no uncreated being except God. God has no opposite. No being could attain a "perfect badness" opposite to the perfect goodness of God; for when you have taken away every kind of good thing (intelligence, will, memory, energy, and existence itself), there would be none of him left.[23]

So who is the Devil? At this point, it would be easy for me to give you the quick Sunday school answer to this question: "He's an archangel who wanted to be God, which resulted in him getting kicked out of heaven." But I'm not sure that's completely accurate, and I'm pretty sure there's a lot more to him than that. That being said, I'll give you some things to consider and leave it to you to draw your own conclusions. I'm going to focus on what we clearly know about Satan:

God created everything (see John 1:3). Therefore, Satan is a created being.

There is only one God (see Deuteronomy 6:4). Therefore, Satan is not God.

Because Satan is not God, he does not know everything, is not all-powerful, and cannot—unlike God—be everywhere at once, which is why he has to "roam" around (see Job 1:7; 1 Peter 5:8).

Satan appears to be an angelic being[24] who abused his free will and became an enemy of God (see Job 1:6-12;

Revelation 12:7-9). In the Bible, Satan is never referred to as an archangel, but if Ezekiel 28:16 is referring to Satan (which I'm not sure it is), then Satan may be a "guardian cherub." Ezekiel 28:11-19 may be referring to Satan—comparing the pride of the King of Tyre with the pride of Satan—or it may just be referring to the King of Tyre who was turned to "ashes . . . in the sight of all who saw [him]" (Ezekiel 28:18). I've studied this passage and have read convincing arguments on both sides. I'm just not sure.

When humans encountered angelic beings, they were always terrified (see Luke 2:10). And when encountered, Satan is also terrifying, like a hungry lion is terrifying (see 1 Peter 5:8)—but he can also appear unterrifying, like an angel of light, as I mentioned earlier, or as a serpent.

Satan, at the beginning of time in the Garden of Eden, took the form of a serpent to tempt Adam and Eve (see Genesis 3:1-15; Revelation 12:9).

With his resurrection, Jesus crushed the serpent's (Satan's) head (see Romans 16:20)—not with a long-handled shovel or a hoe[25], but with his heel (see Genesis 3:15).

Therefore, Satan has lost.

Satan is a loser! The war has been won!

We are not fighting *for* victory; we're fighting *from* victory!

Still, Devotee, as you sit there by yourself, it's important that you know that Satan wants you to lose the battle and miss the eternal victory celebration, so he'll try to isolate you from other Christians because he thinks that you'll be easier to devour when you're alone.

That's why Satan came to Eve when Adam wasn't looking (see Genesis 3:1-6).

That's why Satan came to Job (with God's permission) when he was isolated by grief (see Job 1–2).

That's why Satan came to Jesus while he was alone in the wilderness (see Luke 4:1-13).

Immediately following his baptism, Jesus was led by the Holy Spirit into the wilderness, where for forty days he was tempted by the Devil. During those forty days, Jesus fasted. Have you ever fasted? You should. Fasting is when you don't eat so that you can draw closer to God.[26]

Jesus, as he began his ministry, was using the forty days in the wilderness to draw closer to his Father. His time of waiting, listening, and testing in the wilderness was crucial for the future success of his ministry.

As you begin your relationship with Jesus, you are also in a forty-day period of time that you are setting apart to draw closer to Jesus. This time of waiting, listening, and testing is crucial to the future health of your relationship with Jesus, so it's important that you are prepared for an attack from Satan.

Jesus was in the wilderness alone, so Satan attacked.

Jesus was hungry, so Satan tempted him to use his divine power to turn a stone into a piece of bread. Jesus deflected Satan's attack with Scripture (see Luke 4:3-4).

Jesus was vulnerable, so Satan took Jesus to a high place, showed him all the kingdoms of the world, and tempted him with the power to rule them. Jesus defended himself from Satan's attack with Scripture (see Luke 4:5-8).

Jesus was in a spiritual wilderness, so Satan took him to the pinnacle of the temple and tempted him with the opportunity to experience divine rescue. Jesus drove Satan away with Scripture (see Luke 4:12-13).

In the last chapter I talked about the importance of learning. I want you to notice that Jesus knew Scripture and could recite it when Satan attacked. I also want you to notice that Satan knows Scripture too and tried to use it against Jesus (see Luke 4:9-11). Devotee, it is crucial that you memorize Scripture, read Scripture, and know how to apply it to your life because your enemy is prowling around hoping to catch you alone and with your guard down.

Satan thought Jesus was easy prey because he was alone in the wilderness. Devotee, you need to be prepared for Satan to come to you when you are alone too.

Alone in your grief.

Alone in your pain.

Alone in your confusion.

Alone in your debt.

Alone in your guilt.

Alone at your school.

Alone in your marriage.

Alone in your home.

Alone in your room on the Internet.

Do you understand that I was serious when I said that Satan is prowling around trying to catch you? The Bible also teaches us that Satan is a hungry lion who prowls around looking for "someone to devour" (1 Peter 5:8). He's not looking for "some group" or "some people"; he's looking for isolated prey to devour.

Oh, have you seen that video on YouTube called "Battle at Kruger"?[27] I'm sure you have because, as of right now, it's received over 72.7 million views. The video shows a pride of lions attacking a baby water buffalo after the unsuspecting herd walks right upon the lions. The pride attacks, and in a matter of moments the baby is isolated from the rest of the herd and dragged into a nearby body of water. While in the water, things get even more dramatic when a crocodile approaches, grabs the baby water buffalo and tries to wrestle it away from the lions and into the water. The lions win the tug-of-war and drag the baby water buffalo onto shore to a spot where he can be more easily devoured.

Then at four minutes and thirty seconds into the video, something unexpected happens: The herd comes back into the frame of the video to confront the lions and try to free the baby water buffalo.

WE HAVE AN UNCOMMON HERD . . . I MEAN FELLOWSHIP

Do you know that when you gave your life to Christ and left your old life of sin, your pursuit of self, your old way of thinking, your doubt, your anger, your fear, and your pride, you joined a herd (of sorts)?

You may be sitting there, reading this book, beginning your relationship with Jesus all by yourself, but you are not alone. You are a part of something much bigger than yourself. The Bible describes what you are now a part of as a "church" (1 Corinthians 1:2), a "body" (Ephesians 5:23), a "flock" (1 Peter 5:2), a "household" (Ephesians 2:19), a "city" (Hebrews 12:22), and a "people" (1 Peter 2:10).

The first Christ-followers, of whom we read in Acts 2, didn't just know this truth; they lived this truth, which is evidenced by a word that is used more than any other word in the book of Acts to describe how these Christians lived their lives: *together*.

All who believed in Jesus were "together" (Acts 2:44).

They attended the temple "together" (Acts 2:46).

They remembered Jesus "together" (Acts 2:46).

They prayed "together" (Acts 4:24).

They were gathered "together" in one place that shook because of the power of God's Holy Spirit (Acts 4:31).

They were all "together" in Solomon's Portico (Acts 5:21).

They gathered "together" at Mary's house to pray when Peter was imprisoned (Acts 12:12).

They gathered "together" to praise God for the "door of faith" he opened to reach Gentiles through the work of Paul and Barnabas (Acts 14:27).

They gathered "together" to receive the letter from the Jerusalem Council freeing the new Gentile Christians from the rigid expectations their Jewish brothers were trying to impose on them (Acts 15:30).

They gathered "together" to eat (Acts 20:7).

They gathered "together" to survive (Acts 28:14,15).

These Christ-followers were under attack. Luke records in Acts that Saul, who was later to receive the gospel and become an apostle named Paul, was "ravaging the church, and entering house after house [dragging] off men and women and [committing] them to prison" (Acts 8:3). The church is not a building; it's a group of Christians who are gathered together. Paul was trying to destroy the church by arresting Christians who were gathered together in homes, but he eventually learned that you can't defeat a group of people who understand the power of sticking together.

Last week, at our small group,[28] one of the members of the group asked for prayer for his marriage. Buck is a "man's man" and, by his own admission, not prone to crying, so even he was shocked when the tears began to stream down his cheeks as he spoke of his love for his wife and his concerns for the future of their marriage. He apologized for sharing his burden with us, but we were glad to bear it with him.

We're supposed to bear it with him.

Are you trying to carry your burdens alone? Do you believe you're carrying your burdens alone?

Devotee, Satan wants you to think you're in the wilderness alone, and those rocks you're looking at aren't going away, so you might as well make them palatable and start ingesting them. He wants to show you all the kingdoms of the world and convince you that they are his to give and yours to have if you'll just give in to him. He wants you to question *who* you are and *whose* you are, and he wants you to cast your life from the pinnacle to the pit, where he'll be waiting with open arms.

That's what he wanted of my dear friend Buck.

Buck showed up at our small group last week, lost in the

wilderness, feeling hopeless and alone. Satan thought Buck was easy prey and all alone, but he was mistaken.

The moment Buck finished speaking, we immediately rose up out of our seats, came together, encircled him, laid our hands on him, and prayed for him. As we prayed together with Buck, the rock became an inedible object again, Buck saw the King of all the kingdoms in the world and began to worship him, and he fell into the strong arms of the angels.

It was kind of like what happened at four minutes and thirty seconds into that "Battle at Kruger" video, when the herd came back into the frame of the video to confront the lions and try to free the baby water buffalo. It was astonishing! Just when it looked like the baby water buffalo was about to be devoured, the herd of water buffaloes showed up, walked together toward the lions, and—one by one—chased each lion away until the baby water buffalo was free. Cue the victorious music and fade to black!

Just when Buck thought he was about to be devoured, his herd of Christians showed up, walked together to his side, and—as one—chased the enemy away until he was free. Cue the doxology and the after-small-group snacks!

I just watched the "Battle at Kruger" for the seventeenth time and noticed something I hadn't noticed the previous sixteen times I watched it.

At four minutes and thirty seconds into the video, just as the herd is viewed coming back to rescue their baby, one of the men on the video says, "Now they're going to come and try to chase the lions, but I think they're too late." To which a woman replies, "I think you're right. They're way too late now." Then at four minutes and fifty seconds, another woman can be heard clearly lamenting, "You're too late. You're too late."

But she was mistaken, and you are too, anytime you start to believe that you're all alone, the herd has moved on, and it's too late for you or anyone else to be rescued from the grip of the enemy.

Devotee, you are not alone.

You are a part of the church—the body of Christ.

We must stand against the enemy . . . together.

We must survive the trials of life . . . together.

We must share our lives . . . and our pound cakes . . . together!

CHAPTER 7

REMEMBERING: THE DESCANSO AT MILE MARKER 38

And they devoted themselves to . . . the breaking of bread.

— Acts 2:42

OUR WORSHIP MINISTER, Matt, had lunch with Shawn Yoho that Tuesday to make him a job offer, and we were all excited when he accepted the invitation to join our staff as a worship ministry apprentice. We had grown to love him, and we found out that day that the feeling was mutual. Shawn had been serving with us for several months and had distinguished himself, not just with his musical ability but, more importantly, with his remarkable heart for people and the Lord.

It was Tuesday, January 10, 2012, and just two weeks earlier at our Christmas Eve service, Shawn had delivered the performance of the evening with his version of Andrew

Peterson's "Deliver Us," from the program *Behold the Lamb of God*.

His grandfather was at the concert and heard Shawn play and sing. I can still see the joy radiating on Shawn's face as we stood in the back of the church and his grandfather bragged on him and gushed about how well his grandson sang that song. We all agreed. Shawn and his grandfather smiled as they looked at each other.

It was a great moment to witness.

I can't forget it.

I won't forget it.

I won't forget him.

Shawn Yoho left early the morning after January 10 because the band of which he was a member was to lead worship at a week of camp in California. They were crammed in a Dodge Durango with their instruments, suitcases, and sound equipment. As they traveled west on I-70 out of Colorado and neared Richfield, Utah, they came upon a roadblock. Traffic was stopped while crews cleared power lines that had been clipped by a plane earlier that morning and were now strewn across the highway.

A few seconds later, as Shawn and his fellow band members sat and waited for the lines to be cleared from the highway, they were unexpectedly rear-ended by a vehicle driven by a young man who was under the influence. At this horrific moment, the unthinkable happened: A piece of sound equipment became dislodged during the impact and hit Shawn's head.

Shawn died early on Thursday, January 12, 2012, from a traumatic injury to the head. He was twenty years old.

My family had grown quite attached to Shawn. He was teaching my son to play the guitar, he was on the worship team for our youth group, and he was, according to my eldest son, "A real bro!" I enjoyed being around Shawn and was looking forward to working with him as a member of our worship team. But even more than that, I was looking forward to serving with him as a fellow brother in Christ. We are still grieving his loss, but I know we won't soon forget Shawn because his picture hangs on our refrigerator as a reminder of a wonderful young man who, from our limited perspective, died too soon.

I often stop, look at his picture, and remember him.

Shawn made a big impact on our congregation in a short amount of time. Two couples, whose lives were also touched by Shawn's, stopped when they were traveling west on I-70 a couple of months after his death and hung a little brown cross at the spot of the accident to honor Shawn and to ensure that he'll never be forgotten.

The cross those two couples placed at mile marker 38 on I-70 near Richfield, Utah, in memory of Shawn, is properly known as a *descanso*.

If you've traveled the United States of America by car, you've certainly seen one. The word *descanso* is Spanish for "to rest" and now also refers to a memorial, most often a cross, placed on the side of the road where a person died suddenly or was fatally injured away from home.

Descansos date back to the eighteenth century and have their roots in Hispanic culture and the handling of a casket during a funeral procession. Often, funeral processions would require the pallbearers to carry the casket a considerable distance from the church to the graveyard or burial site. When, on occasion, the pallbearers would need to stop, rest, and set the casket on the ground along the path, out of respect for the deceased and to honor the place of "rest" where the body was set on the ground, mourners in the processional would mark the spot with a small pile of rocks or a small cross fashioned out of sticks.

When that cross was placed at mile marker 38 on I-70 near Richfield, Utah, that spot became sacred—a place to stop and remember Shawn Yoho, a fine young Christian man who died too soon.

It's a descanso—a place to stop and remember Shawn.

When that food was set on that table before those disciples in that Upper Room the night before Jesus' death on that cross, and he instructed them to remember him every time it was eaten, that meal became sacred—a time to stop and remember a Savior who died at just the right time.

It's a descanso—a place to stop and remember Jesus.

There is some difference of opinion regarding whether the "breaking of bread" of which we read in Acts 2:42 is referring to a time of eating unleavened bread and drinking fruit of the vine in remembrance of Jesus (what I'll refer to as "Communion" from here on out), or just regular meals. Based on the fact that "breaking of bread" is set in the context of other key elements of early Christian gatherings, apostles' teaching, fellowship, and prayers, I believe that this is referring to a communion service.

Thus, I believe when we read that the first Christ-followers were "devoted . . . to . . . the breaking of bread" in Acts 2:42, we are reading that they were devoted to resting and remembering the sacrifice of Jesus Christ by eating bread and drinking fruit of the vine in a communion service.

Like always, I'd challenge you to study this issue for yourself (whether Acts 2:42 is referring to a communion service or just a meal) and draw your own conclusions. Remember, a mind is a terrible thing to waste.

I need to pause here and explain why I'm referring to this time of remembrance as Communion. The meal Christ instituted in the Upper Room on the night before his death has most often been referred to with one of the following three terms: Eucharist, Communion, and the Lord's Supper. *Eucharist* is a transliteration of the Greek word for "giving thanks," which is found in 1 Corinthians 11:24: "And when he had given thanks, he broke it, and said, 'This is my body which is for you. Do this in remembrance of me.'" *The Lord's Supper* is a term Paul uses in 1 Corinthians 11:20 in his rebuke of the Corinthian Christians and their abuse of this memorial: "When you come together, it is not the Lord's supper that you eat." The term I prefer, *Communion*, originally came into popular use because it is the word that the translators of the King James Version of the Bible used to describe this meal in 1 Corinthians 10:16: "The cup of blessing which we bless, is it not the communion of the blood of Christ? The bread which we break, is it not the communion of the body of Christ?" I also like the word *Communion* because it communicates at least two important realities of this time of remembrance: When we join together to eat the bread and drink the cup, we are in communion with one another, and we are in communion with God.

And it's impossible to experience true communion without stopping.

STOP

We don't like to stop or even slow down.

Gotta keep working.

Gotta keep texting.

Gotta keep moving. We invented drive-through windows at beverage stores, coffee shops, restaurants, Goodwill stores, drug stores, and churches so we can hydrate, caffeinate, masticate, medicate, donate, and meditate while we navigate at ten miles per hour over the speed limit and never have to evacuate our vehicles, as the good Lord did mandate.[29]

Have we forgotten that meals are so much more important than food?

Meals are important to relationships.

Meals are important to families, so we should stop and eat together. My parents understood this and made family dinnertime a priority as my siblings and I were growing up. Mealtimes in our house fed me with so many precious memories that—even today, decades removed from my seat between my sisters and across from my brother—still satisfy my soul. Eating meals as a family helped us to establish deep and lasting relationships with one another.

Meals are important to couples, so we should stop and eat together. It was over the course of many meals that I really got to know Rhonda. Tables become organic when people take their places around them, connecting to one another in ways previously not realized or imagined. With each meal Rhonda and I shared, we became more connected with each other.

Meals were important to Jesus, so we should stop and eat together. Together with sinners. Jesus stopped and ate with sinners because he knew meals were a powerful and effective way to connect with people and build meaningful relationships.[30] Together with saints. Jesus commanded his disciples to stop, come together, and "do this in remembrance of me."

Do what?

Stop.

In 1840, Alexis de Tocqueville wrote in *Democracy in America* that the American "is always in a hurry. . . . Besides the good things that he possesses, he every instant fancies a thousand others that death will prevent him from trying if he does not try them soon. This thought fills him with anxiety, fear and regret."[31] Sound familiar?

Are you too busy?

I love the story about the working mom who promised her three active sons that she'd play cops and robbers with them after she finished the dinner dishes. Romping around in the backyard, one of the boys aimed his toy pistol at his mom and hollered, "Bang, you're dead," and Mom slumped to the ground. Her next-door neighbor, who was watching them play, noticed that she didn't get up. He became concerned and ran over to see if she had been hurt in the fall. When he bent over, the exhausted mother opened one eye and whispered, "Don't give me away. . . . This is the first chance I've had to rest all day."

I hope you don't have to take a fake bullet to get some rest.

It's okay to stop. In fact, it's more than okay to stop; it's godly.

When creating this world, God stopped (see Genesis 2:2).

God commanded his people to stop each week (see Exodus 20:8).

Jesus stopped throughout his ministry (see Mark 1:35).

Heaven is going to be one big *stop*! (see Hebrews 4:9-10).

Devotee, one of the intrinsic blessings of gathering with other Christians around a table to remember the death, burial, and resurrection of Jesus is the opportunity to stop and rest.

Busyness can hurt our relationships with other people. "Love" can definitely be spelled "T-I-M-E," but it can also be spelled "S-T-O-P." Husbands who love your wives, stop and spend time investing in them the same way Christ invested himself in the church. Wives who love your husbands, stop and spend time investing yourselves in their lives, interests, and needs. Dads and moms who love your kids, stop texting, engage the kids, get off Facebook, pause Candy Crush, forget that last e-mail, and focus on being "present" at home. Too many relationships are silenced by the noise we allow to deafen us to the still, small voices of loved ones leaning in, listening for just a whisper of affection.

Busyness can hurt our relationship with Jesus. Devotee, like a smitten young man who can't take his eyes off the girl across the table, like the blushing bride adoring her groom at the altar, like the couple who can't wait to cuddle on the couch in front of the Christmas tree after the kids go to bed, or like the husband and wife on the park bench who've been married sixty-two years and still can't get enough of each other, I want you to not just love Jesus; I want you to love being in his presence.

I agree with Calvin Miller when he says, "No one who hurries into the presence of God is content to remain for long. Those who hurry in, hurry out."[32]

As you develop your relationship with Jesus, learn the pleasure found only in his presence. Calvin Miller said it this way: "Intimacy with Christ comes from entering his presence with inner peace rather than bursting into his presence from the hassles of life."[33]

I know you're busy, but with Martin Luther say, "I have so much to do that I shall spend the first three hours in prayer."[34] I know you have good works to do, but with Mother Teresa request, "Pray for me that I not loosen my grip on the hands of Jesus under the guise of ministering to the poor."[35]

Communion provides perspective for this life and an opportunity to stop and remember what really matters, which is why Christ commanded, "Do this in remembrance of me."

But remember what?

REMEMBER

Communion is much like the ring on the third finger of my left hand right now. The gold wedding ring I wear is not my marriage, but it's a symbol representing the covenant I made with Rhonda. And it reminds me—whether together or apart—of the promises I made to her before God.

Communion is a symbol representing the covenant Jesus made with us through his death, burial, and resurrection and a reminder that a day is coming when we will eat the emblems of Communion with Jesus in heaven. But I'm getting a little ahead of myself.

Communion can be confusing if you are not aware of the symbolism. The Roman Emperor Nero pointed to Communion as evidence that Christians were practicing cannibalism and used that accusation as fuel to fire up his persecution of the church.

A friend I invited to church when I was a little kid shouted, "Yes, snack time!" when he saw the tray coming his direction. Last Sunday, a middle-school girl whose family (I was told) was at church for the first time in her life, went by one of our Communion stations, grabbed the emblems, and came up to me and one of our prayer counselors at the front of the auditorium with the emblems held up and asked, "What are these?" As the worship service continued, we explained to her what the emblems represented and ended up baptizing her and the other six members of her household that very hour.

As I explained the emblems of Communion to her and remembered, I found myself again in the Upper Room.

It was the night before his crucifixion. Jesus had gathered his disciples to eat the Passover meal. The Passover was both a meal and a celebration on the fifteenth day of the Hebrew month of Nisan (usually March or April) to remember the deliverance of the Israelites from Egypt by God under the leadership of Moses. It was a feast established by God just before the tenth plague (see Exodus 12:14).

The tenth plague, the death of the firstborn (see Exodus 12:29), hastened the release of the Israelites by Pharaoh. At midnight, God passed through Egypt to take the life of all firstborn sons and livestock in the land of Egypt, but since he is a good God, he provided a way through which the people of Israel could be delivered. If they placed the blood of a lamb on the sides and tops of their doorframes, death would pass over them (see Exodus 12:21-27).

So it was the Passover, and Jesus had prepared the Passover meal for his disciples in an upper room. Luke remembers it like this:

And when the hour came, he reclined at table, and the apostles with him. And he said to them, "I have earnestly desired to eat this Passover with you before I suffer. For I tell you I will not eat it until it is fulfilled in the kingdom of God." And he took a cup, and when he had given thanks he said, "Take this, and divide it among yourselves. For I tell you that from now on I will not drink of the fruit of the vine until the kingdom of God comes." And he took bread, and when he had given thanks, he broke it and gave it to them, saying, "This is my body, which is given for you. Do this in remembrance of me." And likewise the cup after they had eaten, saying, "This cup that is poured out for you is the new covenant in my blood." (Luke 22:14-20)

This meal was simple, yet significant.

Unleavened bread.

Fruit of the vine.

"Do this in remembrance of me."

Everything about the Passover was about remembering.

Remembering freedom. Every element of this meal was a testimony to and celebration of freedom, even their posture. They reclined because they were free (reclining at a table was not permitted of slaves).

Remembering sacrifice. They ate unleavened bread to remember they left their homes in Egypt so quickly that the bread they were preparing didn't have time to rise.

Remembering promises. Promises past. Four cups of wine were used in the Passover meal—each cup representing a specific promise made by the Lord and recorded in Exodus 6:6-7.[36]

Everything about this meal with Jesus was about remembering.

Remembering freedom. Those reclining with Jesus at this table would one day sit with him at his table in the kingdom (see Luke 22:28-30), having been delivered from the bondage of sin (see Romans 8:2-11).

Remembering sacrifice. They broke and ate bread without leaven to remember the breaking of a body without sin.

Remembering promises. Jesus calls the fruit of the vine a "new covenant (promise) in my (his) blood" (Luke 22:20). This meal, and the emblems therein, is a promise that everyone who tastes him will not taste death (see John 3:16).

Remembering Jesus.

Do this in remembrance of him.

When we drink the Communion cup, we are remembering the promise found in his shed blood. "This cup that is poured out for you is the new covenant in my blood."

The firstborn of the Israelites were saved from certain death by the smearing of the blood of a lamb over the doorways of their homes. Jesus, the "firstborn of all creation" (Colossians 1:15) and the "Lamb of God" (John 1:29) saved us from certain death by the shedding of his blood on the cross.

In God's mind, blood is essential to the forgiveness of sins. He inspired the writer of Hebrews to note, "Without the shedding of blood there is no forgiveness of sins"

(Hebrews 9:22). When we drink the fruit of the vine during Communion, we are remembering that God forgets the sins of all who, through faith, have applied the blood of Christ to the frame of their hearts. Death passes over the blood-covered hearts of the people of God.

When we eat the communion bread, we are remembering the promise found in his broken body: "And he took bread, and when he had given thanks, he broke it and gave it to them, saying, 'This is my body, which is given for you. Do this in remembrance of me'" (Luke 22:19).

I wonder if Jesus winced when he broke that bread, knowing what was to come. He had a physical body, and it was going to be brutalized and then nailed to a cross. It was going to hurt more than we could ever imagine.

One of the first heresies of the church was the false teaching that Jesus didn't have a physical body while on earth and that, when he rose from the dead, it wasn't a physical resurrection.[37] Jesus did indeed have a physical body which was nailed to a cross, buried in a borrowed tomb, and raised from the dead; therefore, we can have confidence that, if we put our faith in Christ, after our death, our physical bodies will rise again too. Combating this heresy directly, the apostle Paul wrote, "If Christ has not been raised, then our preaching is in vain and your faith is in vain" (1 Corinthians 15:14).

But our faith is not in vain!

Devotee, remember that every time you eat the bread of Communion. Remember that every time you drink the cup of Communion.

Life can be so busy. Don't rush past the Communion table. It was prepared for you by the One who loves you.

With the disciples in the early church, be devoted to the breaking of bread. It's a descanso, of sorts—a place where you can stop and remember. As you develop your relationship with Jesus, love him enough to stop regularly and remember how much he loves you.

I need to tell you a little more about the song that Shawn sang at our Christmas Eve concert, just two short weeks before he died. As I mentioned earlier, Shawn sang the song "Deliver Us" from Andrew Peterson's *Behold the Lamb of God*.

Here are the lyrics to that powerful song:

Our enemy, our captor is no pharaoh on the Nile
Our toil is neither mud nor brick nor sand
Our ankles bear no calluses from chains, yet Lord, we're bound
Imprisoned here, we dwell in our own land

Deliver us, deliver us
Oh Yahweh, hear our cry
And gather us beneath your wings tonight

Our sins they are more numerous than all the lambs we slay
These shackles they were made with our own hands
Our toil is our atonement and our freedom yours to give
So Yahweh, break your silence if you can

Chorus
'Jerusalem, Jerusalem
How often I have longed
To gather you beneath my gentle wings'[38]

_____

If you're ever on I-70 near Richfield, Utah, at mile marker 38, I'd encourage you to stop, find the little brown cross, and remember a young man who once sang these words of deliverance, only to experience them for real two weeks later.

And if you have a copy of Andrew Peterson's *Behold the Lamb of God* CD, I'd encourage you to put it in, press track number four, and remember a Devotee named Shawn and the Deliverer to whom he is eternally devoted.

CHAPTER 8

PRAYING: "I PLEDGE ALLEGIANCE"

And they devoted themselves to . . . the prayers.—*Acts 2:42*

FOR YEARS, it was how I started every day.

With my hand over my heart I'd say, "I pledge allegiance to the flag of the United States of America . . ." I could say it by heart.

I could recite, by heart, the reply my father made us say every time we answered the phone when we were little: "Chambers' residence, Arron speaking."

I could say my prayers by heart: "Dear heavenly Father. Thank you for this wonderful day."

Occasionally, I'd get those mental files crossed, creating some interesting moments. One time, my dad called home and I answered the phone, "Dear heavenly Father . . ." Surprisingly, my allowance went up that week!

Another time, I began the Pledge of Allegiance, "Chambers' residence, Arron speaking." My friend Danny, who was half asleep but heard my proclamation and now was completely disoriented—thinking he had suddenly and miraculously been transported to my house—quipped, "Arron, this ain't your house, and I ain't calling you!"

And yet another time, I began an early-morning, pre-bowl-of-shredded-wheat prayer, "I pledge allegiance . . ." I'm sure God appreciated the impromptu assertion of my devotion, but he was probably a little confused by such a strong verbal commitment from a footie-pajama-clad six-and-a-half-year-old who he knew still struggled with keeping his finger out of his nose and tying his shoes.

"I know that by heart." That's an interesting phrase.

It implies that what you are saying comes from, or is in the very near proximity of, the heart, but—as in my illustrations—we can say things "by heart" that don't come from, by, or anywhere near the proximity of the heart. Like starting a prayer by declaring, "I pledge allegiance." That's great if it's true, but in my situation back then—that morning in those footie pajamas—it wasn't true. It should have been, but I was six and a half years old, and I couldn't know what devotion to Jesus really looked like.

I knew nothing of martyrs.

I knew nothing of crosses.

I knew nothing of loss.

I knew nothing of marital infidelity.

I knew nothing of abuse.

I knew nothing of cancer.

I knew nothing of divorce.

I knew nothing of addiction.

I knew nothing of infertility and miscarriages.

I knew nothing of suicide.

I knew nothing of war.

I knew nothing of Alzheimer's.

I knew nothing of brain tumors.

I knew nothing of herniated disks.

I knew nothing of widowed moms.

I knew nothing of dads dying of heart attacks while preaching at a camp in Ohio.

I knew nothing about anything that could make it hard to pray "I pledge allegiance" to Jesus, but now I do—and I do. I do know what it feels like to pray when you have nothing else but God, and I do now pray with a heart devoted to him.

Are you devoted to Jesus? Are you devoted to praying to him? If your heart was squeezed so that what you truly felt for God oozed up and out through your lips in prayer, would it sound like a pledge of allegiance?

Devotee, as you begin your relationship with Jesus, I pray that your heart will be devoted to Jesus and that your prayers will reflect that heartfelt devotion.

This is how the first Christ-followers prayed. They were devoted to praying.

WHAT IS PRAYER?

Prayer is communication with God.

Communication is the lifeblood of any healthy relationship.

Between spouses.

Between parents and children.

Between friends.

Between us and the Lord.

A man was sure his wife was losing her hearing. To test his theory, the next time he entered the house, he stopped at the screen door and yelled to his wife, who was standing at the sink with her back toward him, "Honey, what's for dinner?"

No response.

He walked into the living room, stood in the middle facing the kitchen, and yelled again, "Honey, what's for dinner?"

Nothing. She didn't even flinch.

He walked to the edge of the kitchen, with his toes touching the linoleum, and yelled, "Honey, what's for dinner?"

Silence.

Finally, he stood right behind her and yelled at the top of his lungs, "Honey, what's for dinner?"

To which she replied, "For the fourth time—chicken!"

If you feel like there are communication problems between you and the Lord, it's not his fault.

He is still in his holy temple (see Psalm 11:4). He never sleeps (see Psalm 121:4). He is everywhere. As the psalmist proclaims,

Where shall I go from your Spirit?
   Or where shall I flee from your presence?
If I ascend to heaven, you are there!
   If I make my bed in Sheol, you are there!
If I take the wings of the morning
   and dwell in the uttermost parts of the sea,
even there your hand shall lead me,
   and your right hand shall hold me.
If I say, "Surely the darkness shall cover me,
   and the light about me be night,"
even the darkness is not dark to you;
   the night is bright as the day,
   for darkness is as light with you. (Psalm 139:7-12)

Yes, if you feel like God is not hearing your prayers, he is definitely not the problem. With the psalmist I proclaim, "I love the Lord, because he has heard my voice and my pleas for mercy. Because he inclined his ear to me, therefore I will call on him as long as I live" (Psalm 116:1-2).

The psalms can teach us so much about prayer because so many of the psalms are prayers. In fact, we read that the first Christ-followers were devoted to "*the* prayers" (Acts 2:42, emphasis added), which seems to suggest that they were devoted to specific prayers.

This might be referring to the psalms.

Dietrich Bonhoeffer notes in his book *Life Together*, "The Psalter is the great school of prayer."[39] In their book *Praying the Psalms with the Early Christians*, Mike Aquilina and Christopher Bailey note, "The Book of Psalms has been the prayer book and the hymnal of God's people for three thousand years. Israel sang the psalms of David in the Temple built by the son of David,"[40] so it's not a surprise that these first Jewish converts to Christianity went to the psalms when they went to their knees. Aquilina and Bailey continue, "In every psalm, they saw a startlingly clear expression of the love they felt for Christ—the love that burned so brightly that they were willing to die for it if that was what Christ called them to do. In the years and the centuries after Pentecost, Christians came to see the psalms as the preeminent prayers of the New Covenant."[41]

"The prayers" may also simply be referring to the traditional Jewish daily prayer times with which these first Jewish Christ-followers would have been so familiar. Faithful Jews were in the habit of praying three times a day: very early in the morning, in the early afternoon, and at sundown. We are told these Devotees were faithfully meeting in the temple (see Acts 2:46) and that Peter and John were going to the temple to pray (see Acts 3:1). "The prayers" to which these first Jewish Christ-followers were devoted very well may have followed some of the Jewish prayer models with which they were familiar, but most certainly now focused on Christ as their promised Messiah.

Devotee, regardless of whether the first Devotees prayed the psalms or not, what's important is that you know they were devoted to communicating with God through prayer.

HOW DO I PRAY?

Do you know how to ride a bike? They say that once you learn, you never forget. I believe that's true. I've searched the Internet, and I can't find any documented cases of anyone forgetting how to ride a bike.

I can remember the day. It was a bright day in Ohio. The air was cool. The gravel driveway was hard, and the bike was ready. It was the red Schwinn with a banana seat. I say "the" red Schwinn because this bicycle had trained my oldest sister, Leigh-Angela, who now rode a yellow ten-speed. And this bicycle had trained Leslie, the next oldest sister, who now rode her bike up and down Stahlheber Road, often without hands. These were my goals, my heroes, my bicycling role models.

Now it was my turn to learn how to ride.

Dad, who believed that the only things of value in life had to be obtained through pain, walked "the" bike to the edge of the gravel driveway . . . and I followed.

I can still remember the feeling of extreme fear mixed with complete excitement as we three (Dad, the bike, and I) raced down the driveway.

Dust flying.

Gravel crunching.

Pride swelling.

Dad pushing.

He pushed the bike and shouted instructions. "Keep pedaling! Hold tight to the handlebars! Turn toward the side—you're falling!"

Then it happened.

I looked back and saw him let go. . . . I was on my own . . . pedal or fall down . . . and then I was on the ground. And even though I had ridden only a few feet, it was a start, and I knew that I had crossed into another realm of life. It was time to pedal or fall down.

Praying is a lot like riding a bike.

START PEDALING

Unless you're going downhill, you have to pedal to keep a bike moving. If you want to ride, you're going to have to start pedaling.

Devotee, if you want to learn how to pray and develop healthy communication with God, you're going to have to just start praying. Don't make it too difficult. Just start talking. No need to be formal. Respectful, yes . . . scared, no. Prayer is a conversation with someone who loves you more than you can ever imagine. It's a conversation with someone who will never be shocked by what you say or what you confess. It's a conversation with someone who has the power to help you, bless you, comfort you, change you, guide you, save you. It's a conversation with someone who knows you because he created you. It's a conversation with the best Father ever. He's proud of you. He's patient with you. He adores you.

So just start talking to him.

It doesn't have to be on your knees, beside a bed, in a church, with hands clasped, or with eyes closed. Those things are all good, but not essential.

Just start praying.

You can start with "Father . . ."; "Lord . . ."; "Abba . . . ," (which means "Daddy"); "Daddy . . . "; or a myriad of other ways, and then just speak your heart—not "by heart." Avoid repeating words and phrases that you don't understand or mean, like saying "Lord Jesus," "Lord God," or "Father God," a gazillion times in your prayer. If you mean to say those phrases, say them, but try to avoid using words as "fillers" in your prayers. Jesus warns against using "vain repetitions" (Matthew 6:7, KJV) or "empty phrases" (ESV). And then, when you've said all you feel like you need to say, you can finish by saying, "Amen," which means, "let it happen." Isn't that cool? I like to say "Amen" when other Devotees pray—out loud— something that I also want to happen. I also like to close my prayers by saying, "In Jesus' name," because I believe there's power in the name of Jesus, because Jesus is the reason we can talk directly to God and don't have to go through anyone else (see Ephesians 3:12; Hebrews 10:19-22), and because Jesus said, "Whatever you ask in my name, this I will do, that the Father may be glorified in the Son. If you ask me anything in my name, I will do it" (John 14:13-14).

And, just like riding a bike, before you know it, you'll be on your way.

KEEP PEDALING

If you stop pedaling your bike, you'll stop and possibly fall down.

Same thing with praying. Once you start praying, keep praying, or you'll become more susceptible to a fall.

I think of this approach to praying like a constant online "chat" session with God in a universal wireless network with unlimited minutes, no dead zones, and no password needed to connect.[42] You can chat with God anytime you want. He's always there. He'll never block you or "turn off chat." So we can do what the apostle Paul calls "pray[ing] without ceasing" (1 Thessalonians 5:17).

This is what Hannah did when she so desperately wanted a son: "As she continued praying before the Lord, Eli observed her mouth. Hannah was speaking in her heart; only her lips moved, and her voice was not heard" (1 Samuel 1:12-13).

This is what Abraham did when he wanted the Lord to spare Sodom: "Then he said, 'Oh let not the Lord be angry, and I will speak again but this once. Suppose ten are found there.' He answered, 'For the sake of ten I will not destroy it'" (Genesis 18:32).

This is what Jesus did on the night before his crucifixion, seeking God's will for the next day: "And he withdrew from them about a stone's throw, and knelt down and prayed, saying, 'Father, if you are willing, remove this cup from me. Nevertheless, not my will, but yours, be done.' And there appeared to him an angel from heaven, strengthening him. And being in an agony he prayed more earnestly; and his sweat became like great drops of blood falling down to the ground" (Luke 22:41-44).

Hannah, Abraham, and Jesus modeled what it means to

"pray without ceasing," and that's what I want for you. Pray when you're driving (eyes open please!), working, resting, playing, preparing to take a test, preparing to be tested, in the midst of being tested, preparing to discipline your kids, preparing to be disciplined, when things are bad and you don't deserve it, and when things are great and you don't deserve it either.

I heard one time that early African converts to Christianity were earnest and regular in private devotions. Each one reportedly had a separate spot in the thicket where he would pour out his heart to God. Over time the paths to these places became well worn. As a result, if one of these believers began to neglect prayer, it was soon apparent to the others. They would kindly remind the negligent one, "Brother, the grass grows on your path."

Devotee, don't let grass grow on your path.

BARRIERS TO PRAYER

There are many barriers that can hinder your prayer life. Let me identify three: busyness, sinfulness, and humanness.

I discussed busyness in the last chapter, so I won't add much more than to say that Satan wants us to be too busy to pray. John Bunyan, the author of the classic *The Pilgrim's Progress* wrote, "He who runs from God in the morning will scarcely find him the rest of the day."[43] I know you're busy. We're all busy, so we must pray in the morning, at noon, in the afternoon, and in the evening, so as not to lose God in the chaos.

Regarding sinfulness, wise Solomon taught, "The sacrifice

of the wicked is an abomination to the Lord, but the prayer of the upright is acceptable to him" (Proverbs 15:8).

David concurred, "If I had cherished iniquity in my heart, the Lord would not have listened" (Psalm 66:18).

Isaiah prophesied, "Behold, the Lord's hand is not shortened, that it cannot save, or his ear dull, that it cannot hear; but your iniquities have made a separation between you and your God, and your sins have hidden his face from you so that he does not hear" (Isaiah 59:1-2).

The apostle Peter warned, "The end of all things is at hand; therefore be self-controlled and sober-minded for the sake of your prayers" (1 Peter 4:7).

John Bunyan also said, "Prayer will make a man cease from sin, or sin will entice a man to cease from prayer."[44] Like a child who knows that he has blatantly disobeyed, we find it hard to talk to God when we feel dirty, guilty, ashamed, and weak, but that's exactly when we need him most. We all sin, and when you do and you feel like turning away from God, don't. Instead, look him in the eyes, and tell him what he already knows and forgave through the shed blood of his Son.

We all sin. We all need forgiveness. Without Christ, we're all lost.

If you don't think you're lost, you're not going to ask for directions.

Every prayer is an acknowledgment of the existence of God. The opposite is true, as well.

Devotee, never take yourself too seriously and start to buy the lie first told in the Garden of Eden—that you run you own life and don't need God. Remember, God's Word teaches, "Pride goes before destruction, and a haughty spirit before a fall" (Proverbs 16:18). Your prayer life will fail if you aren't humble enough to fall to your knees before him.

Devotee, remember what God said after Solomon had finished building the temple of the Lord. God promised, "If my people who are called by my name humble themselves, and pray and seek my face and turn from their wicked ways, then I will hear from heaven and will forgive their sin and heal their land" (2 Chronicles 7:14).

Be still, pure, and humble as you pray and enjoy the forgiveness and healing that only a God who truly exists can truly provide.

Yes, enjoy praying.

ENJOY THE RIDE!

I loved riding my bike as a child. I liked going fast, jumping stuff, riding with no hands, feeling the wind on my face, enjoying the view, riding with friends, and being independent. Have you forgotten how fun it is to ride a bike? When was the last time you rode? I still ride, and I still enjoy it. Riding a bike still makes me feel powerful and free, which is also how I feel when I pray.

The early Christians experienced what I'm talking about. They were devoted to prayer and enjoyed witnessing God's devotion to them. Luke tells us that they were filled with "awe" at the power of God (Acts 2:43).

I'm going to talk more about this in the next chapter, but

let me go ahead and ask, Are you in awe of God? Well, would you be if your prayers rocked your world—if prayer not only brought tangible blessings and expanded what you know of God, but made you feel more alive in every way?

BLESSINGS OF PRAYER

Prayer moves the hand of God and leads to countless blessings. Let me name two: deliverance and power.

Do you need deliverance from anything? Pray!

Peter was released because the Devotees prayed (see Acts 12:5), but they weren't the first who prayed for and found deliverance. Jacob prayed for deliverance from Esau (see Genesis 32:9-12). The Israelites prayed for deliverance from the Egyptians (see Exodus 2:23-24). The Israelites prayed for deliverance from their own sin of serving the Baals (see Judges 10:10). Hezekiah prayed for deliverance from the Assyrian king, Sennacherib (see 2 Kings 19:15-19). Jonah prayed for deliverance from the belly of the great fish (see Jonah 2:1-9).

No, Peter and John were not the first to pray for deliverance, and they must not be the last.

Do you need deliverance from temptation? Pray! (see 1 Corinthians 10:13; 2 Peter 2:9).

Do you need deliverance from evil? Pray! (see Matthew 6:13).

Do you need deliverance from sin? Pray! (see 1 John 1:9).

Do you need deliverance from anything? Call upon the Lord through prayer! "Everyone who calls on the name of the Lord will be saved" (Romans 10:13).

You already know about the power you have when you become a Devotee.

In the movie *The Bear,* a tiny bear cub is adopted by a large Kodiak bear. The Kodiak teaches the cub how to survive. On one occasion the Kodiak protects the cub from a mountain lion. Later the cub is confronted by the mountain lion when the Kodiak is not around. The cub growls, but his growl is weak and the lion is unfazed. Suddenly the lion turns and runs. The camera pans to show the Kodiak standing behind the cub.

Prayer is an opportunity to stand with the Father against everything and to experience his power. The Devotees we read about in Acts 4 were facing threats and persecution from both the Jews and the Romans, so they prayed a declaration of God's power:

> Sovereign Lord, who made the heaven and the earth
> and the sea and everything in them, who through
> the mouth of our father David, your servant, said by
> the Holy Spirit,
>
> "Why did the Gentiles rage,
>   and the peoples plot in vain?
> The kings of the earth set themselves,
>   and the rulers were gathered together,
>   against the Lord and against his Anointed"—
>
> for truly in this city there were gathered together
> against your holy servant Jesus, whom you anointed,

both Herod and Pontius Pilate, along with the Gentiles and the peoples of Israel, to do whatever your hand and your plan had predestined to take place. And now, Lord, look upon their threats and grant to your servants to continue to speak your word with all boldness, while you stretch out your hand to heal, and signs and wonders are performed through the name of your holy servant Jesus. (Acts 4:24-30)

They prayed for God to "stretch out [his] hand," and he did–and rocked their world! (see Acts 4:30).

And when they had prayed, the place in which they were gathered together was shaken. (Acts 4:31)

Devotee, you are never stronger than when you are on your knees. Prayer is an incredible opportunity to experience the power of God. G. Micheal Cocoris said it this way: "When we rely upon organization, we get what organization can do; when we rely upon education, we get what education can do; when we rely upon eloquence, we get what eloquence can do, and so on. Nor am I disposed to undervalue any of these things in their proper place, but when we rely upon prayer, we get what God can do."[45]

So start pedaling, keep pedaling, and enjoy the ride!

Pray.

Don't talk about it, think about it, and plan to do it. Just do it.

Pray.

Your relationship with Jesus will be stronger as you do it.

Pray.

And, not by heart, but with all your heart.

Pray.

Start and end every day with it.

Pray, Devotee, and may every word you share with the Lord sound to our dear heavenly Father like a pledge of allegiance.

CHAPTER 9

BELIEVING: LEAP!

And awe came upon every soul, and many wonders and signs were being done through the apostles.—Acts 2:43

FAITH IS a uniquely personal thing.

No one can make you believe in anything.

It's a choice.

Your choice.

You can see the Grand Canyon and think, "Wow, water is powerful," or you can choose to believe, "Wow! God is powerful!"

You can receive a check in the mail that keeps your financial head "above water" and think, "Wow, unexpected checks are great," or you can choose to believe, "Wow! God is great!"

You can just barely avoid being hit by a truck that ran a red light in front of you and think, "Wow. That was close," or you can choose to believe, "Wow! God is close!"

You can see your child born and think, "Wow! My wife is amazing!" or you can, and should, choose to believe, "Wow! God *and* my wife are amazing!"

God is amazing! Do you agree?

Devotee, I so deeply want you to believe, because I so deeply believe that life without faith is dead.

Jesus died so we could live. Jesus, the one with whom you are now in a relationship, is longing for you to "have life and have it abundantly" (John 10:10). He didn't die so you could learn how to tie your shoes, ride a bike, write in cursive, identify every element on the periodic table by heart, receive a diploma, party a lot, incur a lot of debt, receive another diploma, get a job, get a mortgage, get more debt, pay bills, pay taxes, gain weight, lose weight, gain weight again, watch *Lost* on Netflix, sleep less, work more, spend even more, tweet, pin, post political remarks on Facebook, post "selfies" on Instagram, watch videos of cats singing, playing, dancing, or juggling on YouTube and share every one of them with Arron Chambers because you know how much he hates cats, and . . . many years later die worn out, used up, broken down, and full of regrets!

Devotee, I want you to live a life full of faith! I want you to know that, with Jesus, you will see waters part, giants fall, water gush out of rocks, storms still, nets fill, fire fall, and dead things come alive.

But it's a choice.

Every day we're either growing into more or shrinking into less.

Choose more.

More life. More love. More faith.

Every day, you can choose to believe, or not. Every day you can choose to know that you are not alone, that you are not an accident, and that you are not limited by what you see.

"Faith is the assurance of things hoped for, the conviction of things not seen" (Hebrews 11:1).

I've never seen God, but I'm convicted that he exists and is actively and currently involved in this world and in our lives. And I want that conviction for you because this conviction, this belief, changes everything.

Nothing is unbelievable.

Nothing is unreachable.

Nothing is unachievable.

Nothing is impossible.

I stand on the truth spoken by one who should know, the angel Gabriel. He said, "Nothing will be impossible with God" (Luke 1:37). I want you to begin your relationship with Jesus with a commitment to leaping.

"Jump!"

I heard their cries, but I couldn't move. I was petrified.

It was a rite of passage for every self-respecting eight-year-old boy at the Cleveland pool in Hamilton, Ohio. We all knew that manhood began just off the end of that high dive twenty feet above the surface of that over-chlorinated water.

Jumping off the high dive was a defining moment. To jump and live guaranteed immediate entrance into the world of manhood and the heart of every girl sitting along the edge of the deep end. To not jump was an emasculating decision.

This was a defining moment.

The choice was clear: Leap, or don't leap.

The moment of our birth, the moment of our first step, our first day of school, our conversion, our first love, our graduation, our wedding day, our first grief, the birth of our first child, the death of a loved one, our retirement, and our decision at the end of the high dive are just a few examples of the moments in our lives that define who we are. Mishandled moments can be hard to overcome and can fill our lives with significant physical, emotional, and psychological hurdles to overcome. But if we can learn to anticipate these moments, embrace them, learn from them, and weave them into the fabric of our identity, these moments can make any life meaningful.

This may be a defining moment for you. The moment when you decide to leap into a more extraordinary life in Christ or the moment you decide to play it safe.

What are you going to do? Don't worry. I'm not asking you to jump—at least, not yet. For now, I'm just asking you to keep reading, keep waiting on the Lord, keep learning, keep growing, and keep listening for that moment God tells you it's time to leap.

I was thinking about flying the other day. Not flying in an aircraft—flying like a superhero.

In a lot of my dreams—well, the ones where I'm not at school, underclothed and frantically trying to remember my locker combination—I'm flying, like Superman, and wearing the proper attire. I love Superman.

There are a lot of good superheroes out there who are genuinely super. The Incredible Hulk has superhuman strength and an anger-management issue—that, thankfully, typically works to the benefit of good guys and the detriment of bad people—but he can't fly. Spiderman is a skilled wall climber who is quite the acrobat and can shoot webs out of his wrists, but he can't fly. Batman has incredible toys and great fighting skills, but he can't fly. Wolverine is generally awesome and can slice things to pieces with his blades, but he can't fly. Captain America uses his physical, moral, and patriotic strength to save people's lives, but he can't fly. Wonder Woman, who is wonderful, smart, strong, and beautiful, can't fly without the aid of her invisible jet.

Aquaman . . . nah, he's not a superhero!

But Superman . . .

You can shoot him, but he doesn't die. You can chase him, but you can't catch him. You can try to hold him down, but he'll just fly away.

"It's a bird. It's a plane. No, it's Superman!"

I did some unscientific research in an attempt to discover the keys to flying. I read as many Superman comics as I could get my hands on, watched many episodes of *Adventures of Superman* with George Reeves, and then watched *Superman*, *Superman II*, *Superman III*, *Superman IV*, *Superman Returns*, and *Man of Steel*, and even suffered through a few episodes of *Lois & Clark: The New Adventures of Superman*—and I discovered the three keys to flying, which I'm sharing with you because I want more for you. I want you to have a faith that flies.

DON THE PROPER ATTIRE

The first key to flying is to don the proper attire.

A superhero in a Backstreet Boys concert tour T-shirt, cargo shorts, and sandals may be ready for an afternoon at the mall but is in no way ready to be a superhero. When summoned for service, every self-respecting superhero dons the proper attire—attire more conducive to running, jumping, fighting, and flying.

The first Devotees donned the proper attire when they put on Christ in faith at baptism. Luke tells us that about three thousand people were baptized after Peter's sermon on the Day of Pentecost (see Acts 2:41). The apostle Paul tells us that, when Devotees are baptized, they are getting a lot more than wet; they're donning new attire. To the Devotees in Galatia Paul writes, "For as many of you as were baptized into Christ have put on Christ" (Galatians 3:27).

Devotee, when you put on Christ, you donned the proper attire, so because of your faith in Christ you are ready to take a leap of faith. Just be careful that you also haven't donned the improper attire: sin. Sin for a Christian is like a cape to a superhero. Capes may seem like a good idea, but if you've seen the Disney movie *The Incredibles*, you'll remember the wisdom in Edna's advice to Bob as she reminded him of all of the superheroes who had died because their capes were snagged, caught, or sucked into a jet turbine: "No capes!"

The Hebrew writer words the warning this way: "Therefore, since we are surrounded by so great a cloud of witnesses, let us also lay aside every weight, and sin *which clings so closely*, and let us run with endurance the race that is set before us" (Hebrews 12:1, emphasis added). Sin, like an unwieldy cape, can trip us up, slow us down, keep us from taking a successful leap of faith, and—if not completely set "aside"—get us sucked into an engine called death (see Romans 6:23).

Remember this, Devotee, and you'll be prepared for any and all leaps of faith: No sin! You've put on Christ; don't put on sin.

EXPECT TO FLY

It's one thing to don the proper attire, but if one wants to fly, one has to expect to fly. If you're not expecting to fly, what's the point of the costume? If you're not expecting God "to do immeasurably more than all we ask or imagine" (Ephesians 3:20, NIV), what's the point of putting on Christ?

Devotee, I want you to want more.

I want you to ask for more.

I want you to imagine more.

I want you to expect to fly!

It's not arrogance. You're not God. It's confidence. He is God!

The Christ-followers we read of in Acts were in "awe" because they were experiencing "many wonders and signs" (Acts 2:43). Their faith was growing with each demonstration of the power of God. I want the same for you. You've put your faith in Christ—now put your faith in God to take you higher.

Do you believe that God is capable of "wonders and signs"? Regardless, he is.

When you're in love with someone, it's common to believe the person is capable of supernatural things. As you speak of your loved one, friends and family may protest, "He doesn't walk on water." Well, your Loved One does walk on water.

Your Loved One made the water! You've put on Christ—now embrace the reality and the possibilities!

Believe Christ has taken you beyond your sin.

Believe Christ has taken you beyond your guilt.

Believe Christ has taken you beyond the grave.

Believe Christ can take you beyond anything you're going to face today, tomorrow, and all the days after tomorrow.

Do you love Jesus? If so, you'll also believe in him. It's impossible to truly love someone in whom you don't believe.

I can't imagine being in a relationship with someone in whom you have no faith. If you are single and you're in that kind of relationship right now with another person, save yourself and your future marriage counselor a lot of trouble and break it off—because there's no hope if there's no faith. I believe in my wife. I trust her. She's not perfect—and neither am I—but she's good, truthful, and faithful. I have faith in her, so there is always hope for the future and the expectation that together, we will fly.

In your relationship with Christ, expect him to provide supernaturally for your needs. Expect him to do what you are unable to do.

Build the ark, expecting him to send the flood.

Put it all on the altar, expecting him to send the fire.

Lay it all out before God, expecting him to moisten the fleece (see Judges 6:36-40).

Climb out of a perfectly good boat, expecting not to sink.

In your relationship with Christ, don the proper attire and expect to fly.

The Bible is full of men and women who expected God to do what they were unable to do:

- Abraham was told that he was going to be the father of "a great nation," while he and his wife were dealing with infertility (see Genesis 12:2). After trying to help God with his plan by sleeping with Hagar, he and Sarah were blessed to have descendants as numerous as the stars in the sky (see Genesis 22:17).
- Abraham put Isaac on an altar, trusting that God would save or resurrect his son (see Genesis 22:9).
- Moses didn't think he could talk to Pharaoh, but God used him to deliver an entire nation of people out of bondage (see Exodus 14:30,31).
- Gideon was afraid. God found him hiding in a winepress, yet God used him to defeat a mighty army (see Judges 7).
- David stood before Goliath with only a slingshot and five stones, expecting God to do a miracle (see 1 Samuel 17:49).

- Jeremiah felt inadequate, but God stepped in and used him to make a difference in this world (see Jeremiah 1:6-8).
- Mary was afraid. But still she answered the call to be the mother of our Lord, and God did what she was unable to do (see Luke 1:27-38).
- Peter was afraid, but still he got out of the boat and walked on the water toward Jesus (see Matthew 14:22-33).

Yes, every one of these people did what I want you to do next . . . leap!

LEAP!

Devotee, in your relationship with Christ, a time will come when he will call you to go to the end of the diving board, get on the red Schwinn on the gravel driveway, get out of the boat, and leap, because that's the most important key to flying. To fly you must resist the gravitational pull of facts, figures, fear—and take a flying leap.

If you've ever been to the circus, you've probably seen a huge elephant held in place by a small chain.

Chaining an elephant isn't as simple as just putting a chain around its leg—an adult elephant would snap that chain without even noticing the effort.

The way to chain an elephant is to start when it's

a baby. You don't even need a chain—a strong rope will do.

The baby elephant will struggle, but eventually it will realize that it can't break the rope, and even worse, continuing to struggle creates a painful burn on its leg. The baby elephant learns not to struggle—it accepts that the limit imposed by the rope or chain is permanent, and there is no use struggling against it.

Sure, the elephant grows up and becomes the most powerful land mammal on the face of the earth. But the chains in its mind remain, and so the chains on its leg are never broken.[46]

You need to know that Satan doesn't want you to take a leap of faith.

He'll try to shackle you with facts: "That doesn't make sense!"

He'll try to shackle you with figures: "You need money!"

He'll try to shackle you with fear: "You can't leap!"

But you need to remember that you are not in a religion with a set of rules; you are in a relationship with a powerful Ruler!

- A Ruler with the power to heal a man who had been unable to walk since birth (see Acts 3:1-11).
- A Ruler with the power to strike cheaters dead (see Acts 5:1-10).

- A Ruler with the power to heal a man who had been paralyzed for eight years (see Acts 9:33-34).
- A Ruler with the power to raise a woman from the dead (see Acts 9:36-41).
- A Ruler with the power to release Peter from prison (see Acts 12:7-17).
- A Ruler with the power to heal a man who had been crippled from birth (see Acts 14:8-10).
- A Ruler with the power to release Paul and Silas from prison (see Acts 16:25-26).
- A Ruler with the power to raise Eutychus back to life (see Acts 20:9-12).
- A Ruler with the power to do "many wonders and signs," filling the first Christ-followers with "awe" (Acts 2:43).
- A Ruler with the power to help you to "mount up on wings like eagles" (Isaiah 40:31).

God was doing wonders and signs through the apostles to awe saints and intrigue sinners. Like a spotlight shining brightly in the darkness, the purpose of these miracles was to point people to Jesus and the gospel.

Devotee, live an awe-inspiring life—a life that points people to Jesus. There is nothing awe-inspiring about a person in a costume simply standing on the edge of a cliff, refusing to jump. As a matter of fact, that's a pretty pathetic scene. But there's nothing more awe-inspiring than seeing a person, dressed appropriately, standing on the edge of an opportunity . . . who leaps.

> When Wernher von Braun headed the Marshall Space Flight Center, he received letters from all over the world and had a number of secretaries to compose standard replies. Sometimes von Braun would scribble a few words in the margins of these "form letters." On one occasion, a college student wrote asking about the future of space flight; the secretaries wrote a cautious and formal reply, pointing out the risks, boredom and uncertainties of this new field, suggesting that the student consider all alternatives. Von Braun scratched through the cautious reply and scribbled, "Come with us! We're going to the moon!"[47]

Devotee, let's not live safe, cautious lives. Let's go to the moon!

Resolve that, when God calls, you'll be willing to attempt something so impossible that unless God is in it, it is doomed to fail. Join me in calling out to other Devotees, "Come with us! We're taking off and launching into the heavens!"

I think it would be cool if one day someone would take note of your faith and, in awe, say, "It's a bird! It's a plane! No, it's (insert your name here)!" And that will happen if—with obedient faith—we don appropriate clothing, expect to fly, and leap.

CHAPTER 10

SACRIFICING: "OR, BUY MYSELF A CAR!"

And all who believed were together and had all things
in common. And they were selling their possessions and
belongings and distributing the proceeds to all, as any
had need.—Acts 2:44-45

SACRIFICING DOES NOT come naturally to human beings.

We arrive in this world self-centered. In the crib it is all about us, as it should be. We are the center of the universe, at least as far as we're concerned. Which is okay, because we can't feed ourselves, clothe ourselves, move ourselves, or do anything for ourselves except cry out with the hope that others will rush in and take care of all our needs.

Sadly, some seem to never grow out of this stage. Oh, they may have mastered feeding, clothing, and moving themselves, but some—like infants in a crib, late at night, and with a twinge of craving deep within—still cry out and expect everyone else to rush in and take care of all their needs, which I find pathetic, unnatural, and unscriptural.

The apostle Paul teaches that we Christ-followers "are to grow up in every way" (Ephesians 4:15), and one sure sign that we have grown up is a willingness to sacrifice for others.

Selfishness is a sign of immaturity.

Children must be taught to share, which I thought was a universally accepted truth, but to my surprise, I found an article that made me doubt Canada's support of my thesis. It was the title that caught my attention: "5 reasons why I don't force my kids to share."[48] Now, Maria Lianos-Carbone has some good thoughts about sharing, but she also discusses ideas that seem to me to be . . . well . . . I dunno—how should I say it?—somewhat ludicrous!

That being said, I've decided that her article provides a nice outline of the five reasons newborn christians should be taught to share.

YOUNG KIDS AREN'T WIRED TO UNDERSTAND SHARING

Lianos-Carbone says we shouldn't force kids to share because young kids aren't wired to understand sharing. Young kids also aren't wired to understand not pooping in their pants, but we potty train them, don't we? Yes, young kids don't understand sharing, which is why we teach them to share. But this article only serves to make my point: Sharing doesn't come naturally to human beings, especially young ones.

Newborns are selfish. They don't understand sharing. So as the babies grow, they must be taught the value of sharing things with others. For newborns, it's all about newborns. It has to be.

But as we grow, we can be taught to share.

Devotee, start now to learn that it's not all about you. It never has been about you. It can't be. It's always only been about Jesus.

As you begin your new life in Christ and people like me come to your side to feed you God's Word, clothe you in Christ, and move you to a deeper love for Jesus, receive it. Take it all in. You are an infant in Christ. Eat. Grow. Mature. Take in as much as you can of the fullness of God, not to become engorged on pride, piety, or a twisted pharisaical sense of self-importance, but to have more special stuff to share.

SOME THINGS ARE JUST TOO SPECIAL TO SHARE

The next reason Maria Lianos-Carbone gives for not forcing young kids to share is because some things are just too special to share. She believes if your child doesn't want to share his special toy with his friend, you should avoid the drama and not force him to share.

However, some things are too special *not* to share.

There was an elderly couple who went to a fast-food restaurant. They ordered one cheeseburger, one large fry, one large drink, and an extra soda cup. When the couple sat down, the man sitting next to them watched the man cut the burger in half, divide the fries and give his wife half, and pour the soda in the extra cup he ordered.

The man at the next table was confused, so he went over there and told the couple that if they couldn't afford a meal for each of them, he would be happy to pay for it. The older man shook his head and told him that there was no need because he and his wife had shared everything for the last forty years.

The man went back to his seat, and then he saw the older man eating while the woman just sat there doing nothing.

He went over to them again and asked the lady why she wasn't eating. She said, "Well, it's his turn to use the teeth."

Teeth would fall into the category of things that are too important not to share, but so would anything that would be a blessing to another person. The early Christ-followers knew this, so as we read earlier, they were sharing "all things" (Acts 2:44). When one Christian had a need, another Christian would sell land he owned or the house he was living in (see Acts 4:34) and share the proceeds with the one in need.

As you grow in your relationship with Christ, please know that sharing is a sign of spiritual maturity.

FORCING KIDS TO SHARE ISN'T COOL

The article continues with the admonition that forcing kids to share "isn't cool." Well, as a marriage coach who has worked with hundreds of couples, I'd like to point out that being in a relationship with an adult who was not forced to share as a child is really not cool. Selfishness is kryptonite to a healthy marriage—slowly breaking hearts, crushing dreams, and choking love to death, which is one of the reasons the picture of Christlike love is of a man hanging on a cross.

In Ephesians, the apostle Paul admonishes husbands,

Love your wives, as Christ loved the church and gave
himself up for her, that he might sanctify her, having
cleansed her by the washing of water with the word,
so that he might present the church to himself in
splendor, without spot or wrinkle or any such thing,
that she might be holy and without blemish. In the
same way husbands should love their wives as their
own bodies. (5:25-28)

This is what love looks like: It looks like Jesus sacrificing
his life for us.

Love also looks like us sacrificing our lives for each other,
which contradicts the next bit of wisdom found in the article
to mothers on sharing.

SETTING BOUNDARIES WITH SIBLINGS IS IMPORTANT

Maria Lianos-Carbone proposes that it is important to set
boundaries with siblings regarding their possessions, so a
child is never forced to share something he or she does not
want to share.

This philosophy is so bizarre to me and would have never
worked in our home when I was growing up with my three
siblings. My brother, Adam, and I had to share almost everything when we were little—a room, a closet, dressers, our
toys, a bed (bunk bed), the bathtub (when we were *really*
little), the TV (back in my day, most houses had only one

TV), and boxes of cereal and the "treasure" they used to put in the bottom of said boxes of cereal. When we'd protest having to share with one another, Dad would simply reply, "Brothers share."

Brothers in Christ do share. At least, they do when they love each other.

John Washington loved his brother, Booker. Booker T. Washington was born a slave. After he was freed, he headed the Tuskegee Institute and became a leader in education. When speaking and teaching, he often told of what he called, "the most trying ordeal that I was forced to endure as a slave boy—the wearing of a flax shirt."[49] In Virginia it was common to use flax as part of the clothing for the slaves. They used the worst flax, so when the shirt was new and stiff it was torturous—like wearing a shirt of small thorns. Booker said that he had no choice but to wear the shirt. One time, when Booker was struggling with the reality of donning the painful apparel, his older brother, John, stepped in and generously agreed to wear a new flax shirt for Booker until it was broken in.

That's love.

Love sacrifices.

John, the one "whom Jesus loved" (John 13:23), wrote, "By this we know love, that he laid down his life for us, and we ought to lay down our lives for the brothers. But if anyone has the world's goods and sees his brother in need, yet closes his heart against him, how does God's love abide in him?" (1 John 3:16-17).

The first Christ-followers lived this out, and it looked like them selling land and houses and giving away all the proceeds to help each other. They loved each other. How do I know? Because they shared with each other sacrificially.

Love is sharing.

Love is sacrifice.

It would be uncool if God had to force you to share. That's what made what we see in the lives of the Christians in Acts 2 so cool! This wasn't Communism. They weren't being forced to sacrifice for one another. This was Christianity. They were sacrificing for one another because they wanted to and because they wanted to be like Jesus.

In his letter to the Christians in Philippi, the apostle Paul gives us a powerful look behind the curtain between this world and the heavenlies and allows us a glimpse of what really happened when Christ came to earth as a baby:

Do nothing from selfish ambition or conceit, but in humility count others more significant than yourselves. Let each of you look not only to his own interests, but also to the interests of others. Have this mind among yourselves, which is yours in Christ Jesus, who, though he was in the form of God, did not count equality with God a thing to be grasped, but emptied himself, by taking the form of a servant, being born in the likeness of men. And being found in human form, he humbled himself by becoming obedient to the point of death, even death on a cross. (Philippians 2:3-8)

Sacrifice came naturally to Jesus. It was in his DNA, so he didn't have to be forced to share.

Christ arrived in this world sacrificially—leaving the glory of God's presence to be born in an animal's feeding trough. His crib, that trough, was all about us.

Jesus was God. With God, he had everything.

Jesus became man. As man, he had nothing.

Jesus left the crib for the cross.

Jesus gave up everything for others and wants us to be willing to do the same, which completely goes against Maria Lianos-Carbone's final bit of guidance in regards to little kids and sharing.

NOT EVERYTHING SHOULD BE SHARED

Finally, Maria Lianos-Carbone teaches that kids should not be forced to share everything, which I think makes perfect sense when negotiating the possible sharing of colds, already chewed gum, lice, underwear, used tissues, toothbrushes, and a litter of kittens between children, but contradicts the example of Christ and teachings of Scripture when negotiating the possible sharing of everything between children of God.

Paul writes, "Let each of you look not only to his own interests, but also to the interests of others" (Philippians 2:4). These Christians about whom we read in Acts were living this out. They "had all things in common" (Acts 4:32, KJV) and "were selling their possessions and belongings and distributing the proceeds to all, as any had need" (2:45). They were sharing everything with each other.

Let's look again at Acts 4: "There was not a needy person among them, for as many as were owners of lands or houses sold them and brought the proceeds of what was sold and laid it at the apostles' feet, and it was distributed to each as any had need" (verses 34-35).

The apostles were taking up offerings to help those in need, but they were also taking up offerings from Christians because that's what God wants us to do. He knows it's good for us to share. *Offerings* in this context are monies willingly given by people to help fund the work of the church in this world. In your relationship with Jesus, you will also hear the terms *tithe* and *tithing*. These terms come from the Old Testament and refer to the requirement under the Law of Moses for people to give to the Lord ten percent (a "tithe") of everything they earned or grew (see Leviticus 27:30; Numbers 18:26; Deuteronomy 14:24; 2 Chronicles 31:5).

Under the New Covenant, Christians are no longer required to give a tithe to God, but we are taught specifically to set aside a portion of our income for the Lord (see 1 Corinthians 16:1-2), and we are taught by example that we should be willing to give everything to the Lord, if that's what he leads us to give (see Acts 2–4).

At one point in his ministry, Jesus encountered a man who had everything this world had to offer, but he lacked the most important thing: a willingness to sacrifice for Jesus. Here's Matthew's version of their conversation:

And behold, a man came up to him, saying, "Teacher, what good deed must I do to have eternal life?" And he said to him, "Why do you ask me about what is good? There is only one who is good. If you would enter life, keep the commandments." He said to him, "Which ones?" And Jesus said, "You shall not murder, You shall not commit adultery, You shall not steal, You shall not bear false witness, Honor your father and mother, and, You shall love your neighbor as yourself." The young man said to him, "All these I have kept. What do I still lack?" Jesus said to him, "If you would be perfect, go, sell what you possess and give to the poor, and you will have treasure in heaven; and come, follow me." When the young man heard this he went away sorrowful, for he had great possessions. (Matthew 19:16-22)

Devotee, learn to give. I know you're just a newborn and just beginning your relationship with Christ, but start giving now—to God and to others. Leave the crib, and take up the cross. Remember it's always about others. Be generous with the possessions of God. Hold loosely in your hands the things of this world. Materialism will try to seduce you and convince you to follow, but don't—especially if it starts to lead you away from Jesus. If you give in and choose earthly "treasures" over treasure in heaven, you'll only end up walking away sad.

Your passion for Jesus will always be tested with passions for the stuff of this world.

Last year, my personal assistant's young daughter came

to our staff meeting with her mom, Stephany. Most of our meeting was devoted to a discussion of our current series in which we were calling the church to identify and do a great work for God (based on Nehemiah 6:3). Being at our meeting and hearing us talk about a great work got the little girl's mind reeling. After our meeting, she told her mom that she was going to do a great work. She said, "I think I'll have a garage sale and sell my stuff." Stephany asked her daughter what she would do with the money to make it part of a "great work," to which her daughter replied, "I think I'll put it in the offering." Stephany said she was feeling quite proud until Phoebe finished her sentence: ". . . or, buy myself a car!"

Sacrificing doesn't come naturally to human beings, so we must be intentional with giving our everything to God. Just ask Jesus hanging on that cross or my personal assistant's daughter.

Do you love Jesus? If so, give. This is why the early Christ-followers gave. They were devoted to Jesus.

Are you grateful for the fact that Jesus died on a cross for you? If so, give. Don't stand at the foot of the cross and toss Jesus your loose change.

Do you believe Jesus is coming back again? If so, give now. This is why the early Christ-followers gave when they did. They believed that Jesus was coming back, at any moment, and in anticipation of his return, they didn't want to get too entangled in or distracted by the stuff of this world. They believed Jesus when he said, "And if I go and prepare a place for you, I will come again and will take you to myself, that where I am you may be also" (John 14:3).

If Jesus could come back before I finish writing this sentence and you were in need of a few bucks to survive until he came, why wouldn't I give it to you? What good is money in the bank when Jesus is coming in the clouds? What good is it to say, "I love you, Jesus," if we are not willing to sacrifice for him?

Oh, speaking of buying oneself a car, last spring I had dinner with a man and his wife who had purchased a beautiful and rare Mercedes-Benz. He told me that he enjoyed driving it to church on Sunday mornings and on special occasions, but that most of the time it sat under a tarp in his garage.

He then reminded me of a recent sermon I had delivered on giving entitled "Trash or Treasure?" In that sermon I showed pictures of objects and asked the congregation to identify whether the pictures showed examples of "trash" or "treasure." In the series of pictures, I showed an image of the exact car he had at home under a tarp in his garage. When the picture of his car came up on the screen, the congregation yelled, "Trash!" He told me that he knew that God was telling him right then that he was supposed to sell that car and give the money to the church.

At that point during dinner, his wife pulled a check out of her purse and handed it to her husband, and he slid it across the table, saying, "This is for the church."

It was an unbelievable amount of money.

It was a supernatural moment.

I began to cry. His eyes welled up with tears too.

As I thanked him for making such an extraordinary sacrifice, with a smile he simply confessed, "I just love Jesus!"

Do you just love Jesus? If so, sell that car, write that check, host that garage sale, share that treasure at the bottom of the box of cereal, and give.

Give until it becomes natural.

Give until it becomes supernatural.

CHAPTER 11

ENJOYING: WAIST-DEEP IN UNEXPECTED JOY

*And day by day, attending the temple together and breaking
bread in their homes, they received their food with glad and
generous hearts.—Acts 2:46*

I WAS ABOUT two-thirds of the way through this chapter and
on pace to finish this book a week ahead of schedule when
my plans were washed away by what the National Weather
Service has called a flood of "biblical" proportions.[50]

Late on Wednesday, September 11, it started to rain here
in Northern Colorado . . . and it kept raining. By Thursday
night the lakes, reservoirs, damns, rivers, and creeks in the
Rocky Mountains (just west of where I live) were full, over-
flowing, and no longer containable. That mountain water,
seeking its own level, began flowing down from the high
country and through the streets of mountain towns like Estes
Park, Glen Haven, and Lyons with devastating consequences.

Bridges were wiped out.

Roads were washed away.

Businesses were immersed beneath several feet of muddy water.

Homes were devoured by the rushing torrents and spat out in pieces many miles from where they once stood.

Dreams were doused.

Lives were lost.

Friday the thirteenth was a dreadful day in our community as we awoke to a deluge of heartbreaking stories of loss, images of the shattered infrastructure of our region, and floodwaters now rising in the two rivers that embrace our community from the north and the south and converge on the east side of town.

When the rain stopped, over 1,900 square miles of Northern Colorado across 17 counties had been flooded. Over 1,800 homes were completely destroyed and over 16,000 were damaged. Over 200 miles of road and 50 bridges were destroyed, and 7 people had died, with another 82 souls unaccounted for.[51]

Even so, joy walked in and sat on the back row of church last Sunday night.

"OH, HOW I LOVE JESUS!"

A wise man once said, "Joy is the most infallible sign of the presence of God," which, to me, is evidence that God attended and enjoyed Sunday evening services at West Side Church of Christ in Hamilton, Ohio, in the early 1970s.

My dad was the preacher at West Side for thirteen years. I was eight years old when we left Ohio, so all my memories of that church are from when I was very young. Some of my most precious memories are of Sunday night church services. I loved Sunday night services at West Side. At that time, most churches had two distinct services on Sundays, one in the morning and one at night. To me, Sunday night services always had a different, but comforting, feel to them.

Like sitting around the living room with a bunch of close friends after the guests have left—shoes off, feet tucked up under you as you sit on the couch, relaxed with no pretense or formality—just enjoying each other's company.

The Sunday night crowd was always smaller, but it was made up of a lot of either Devotees who loved going to church or "De-guilt-ees" who hated feeling guilty for staying home on Sunday nights to watch *The Wonderful World of Disney, 60 Minutes*, or the annual showing of *The Wizard of Oz* on network television.

My dad took a more relaxed posture too. No coat. No tie. Clothed in joy.

Back in my day, the pastor had to do pretty much everything at the church. He was the preacher, Sunday school teacher, janitor, church van driver, secretary, and worship director. So on special Sunday nights, my dad—to get a break and to add some variety—would designate Sunday night worship as "Special-Request Night," which meant we could request to sing our favorite songs or choruses.

"Special Request Night" was always a hit with us kids

because we'd get a chance to sing our favorite songs out of the *Favorite Hymns of Praise* hymnbook: #470, "Wonderful Grace of Jesus," #500, "When the Roll Is Called Up Yonder," and my favorite Sunday night song, "Oh, How I Love Jesus," which wasn't in the hymn book because it was a "chorus"—something only recently welcomed into the liturgy of the most "progressive" churches and typically only tolerated on Sunday nights.

Thankfully, West Side was a loving and grace-filled gathering of Devotees who just loved to sing of our love for Jesus—and we loved to sing, "Oh, How I Love Jesus."

From the stage, as we started that song, my dad would sing out a question to one of us kids in the youth group: "Oh, Arron, do you love Jesus?"

To which I'd reply, "Oh yes, I love Jesus!"

Then Dad would sing out another question, "Do you really love Jesus?"

"Yes, I really love Jesus," I'd reply.

Dad would make one more request: "Tell me why you love Jesus."

And the last reply before we all broke into "Oh, How I Love Jesus," was "Because he first loved me."

"Oh, how I love Jesus. Oh, how I love Jesus. Oh, how I love Jesus, because he first loved me!"

Oh, how I loved singing that song, and I loved growing up in that church.

Oh, how I love Jesus.

My dad was intentional about making gatherings of the

church also an amassing of joy. My memories of church are joy-filled ones. We laughed a lot, and that was not only okay, it was expected. Don't get me wrong. My dad preached the Word of God and we were reverent, but Dad didn't just preach Paul's words; he expected us to live them out as a congregation: "Rejoice in the Lord always" (Philippians 4:4).

Devotee, be joyful. Always.

JOY, EXUBERANT

The English Standard Version of the Bible has Luke telling us that the first Devotees to Christ had "glad" hearts (Acts 2:46). Well, that's not really what Luke is telling us because the Greek word he used for "glad" implies so much more than happiness. Literally, Luke wrote that they had hearts that were filled with "exuberant joy,"[52] and there's a big difference between happiness and exuberant joy.

I once heard a preacher say, "Happiness shows up when expected, but joy shows up whenever it wants."

Happiness shows up at birthday parties, weddings, when you get a raise, when you get a good parking space, when you pick the quickest checkout line at the grocery store, when your favorite team wins, and when your wife makes stuffed shells. But joy can show up at the strangest times. Joy can show up while you're watching your kids play on the playground, or while you're eating at your desk and your eyes land on a picture of your spouse, or when you're at a funeral, or when you're stuck in a traffic jam, or when you're forty-four years old, sitting at a desk in the back of your house, working on your sixth book, and remembering a "Special-Request Night" from thirty-six years ago.

Joy shows up whenever it wants to, because joy is not an emotion. Joy is not dependent on our emotions for its existence. Joy is an attitude that knows everything is going to be okay because God is in charge.

Satan is not in charge.

When Jesus declared, "It is finished" (John 19:30), he was really telling Satan, "You are finished!" "The tribe has spoken!" "You are the weakest link, good-bye!" "You've been eliminated from the race!" and "You're fired!"

Yet Satan is not going down without a fight. He's a skilled murderer who wants to kill your hope, dreams, self-esteem, confidence, peace of mind, and joy (see John 10:10). Yes, Satan is the epitome of a killjoy, and he'll use whatever he can to try to kill joy when it shows up unexpectedly at your door. Devotee, I want you to be joyful, so I want you to be prepared.

These new Christ-followers, about whom we read in Acts 2, were devoted to Christ and delirious with joy as they began their new lives in Christ. If verses 42-47 of Acts 2 were an Instagram picture, the caption would read, "Following Jesus is awesome!" Yet don't be ignorant of the world in which they were living and the suffering that stalked them at every move.

SUFFERING, EXPECTED

The first Christians were not living in a world conducive to Christianity.

They didn't get Sundays off so they could go to church.

Their rulers didn't close every speech with "God bless Jerusalem."

There were no prayers to the one true God before kickoff at the coliseum or before graduation ceremonies at the local state school.

There wasn't a Christian bookstore in their local mall where they could load up on WWJD bracelets and Jesus bobblehead dolls they could affix to their dashboards.

There was no radio station that played "Big House" a thousand times a day and other music that was "safe for the little ears" in the backseat.

Their money didn't have "In God We Trust" inscribed on it.

They didn't expect the government-run schools to include a chapter on "Intelligent Design" in the school board–approved science textbook.

They weren't offended when they sneezed and no one responded with, "God bless you!"

They didn't even have Chick-fil-A!

And the crosses on the side of their roads weren't little, white, and adorned with beautiful flowers; they were big, brown, and adorned with the bleeding bodies of people deemed by the Roman government to be criminals.

The first Christ-followers maintained no naive expectation that the government or their bosses would make it easier for them to follow Christ. They were living in a hostile world, wearing the name of a man who was considered by the Romans to be a criminal and by the Jewish leaders to be a heretic.

They saw the world not as a friend and suffering not as a stranger.

They lived, worshipped, broke bread, and received their food with the image of their crucified leader still hanging in their collective memories, yet Luke reveals that they also lived, worshipped, broke bread, and received their food with "glad and generous hearts" (Acts 2:46). They were joyful in the midst of suffering, but as I've already pointed out, they weren't just joyful—they were exuberantly joyful.

Joy shows up whenever it wants, and so does exuberant joy. But when exuberant joy shows up, it also kicks open the door! Especially when it knows Christ's beloved are suffering inside, which is what we see in Acts 5.

Luke records that the Jewish high priest arrested the apostles and put them in prison, but "during the night an angel of the Lord opened the prison doors and brought them out" (Acts 5:18-19).

Now, let me pause here and point out what did and didn't happen next.

What didn't happen is that as quickly as possible the now-free apostles ran as far away from the prison where they had suffered, renouncing their faith in a Savior who refused to save them from the shackles. What did happen is that the now-free apostles obeyed the angel of the Lord's command to "Go and stand in the temple and speak to the people all the words of this Life" (Acts 5:20).

They didn't run from suffering; they walked toward it faithfully.

Beloved, don't run from suffering. Expect it. Embrace it. Exuberantly rejoice as you endure it.

The apostles stood in the temple and preached the gospel faithfully (see Acts 5:25). They were arrested again and brought before the high priest again and were reprimanded for their disobedience, yet they saw this not as an opportunity to throw a pity party but as an opportunity to preach the gospel, resulting in their being beaten (see Acts 5:40).

They were beaten.

Have you ever been beaten?

If Acts 5:40 were an Instagram picture, the caption would read, "Ouch!"

They suffered. They rejoiced.

Luke tells us that they left the place where they'd been beaten "rejoicing that they were counted worthy to suffer dishonor for the name" (Acts 5:41).

NONE EXEMPTED

Devotee, your relationship with Jesus does not exempt you from suffering; it guarantees it.

Are you expecting to suffer in this life? You should. Jesus guarantees us that we are going to suffer. He said, "I have said these things to you, that in me you may have peace. In the world you will have tribulation" (John 16:33). In our relationship with Jesus we are going to experience exuberant joy, but we're also going to experience exhausting sorrow.

Jesus was not unfamiliar with suffering. If there's anyone

who could have played the "victim" card and asked, "Why me?" it was Jesus.

His mother was an unwed, pregnant teen. He was born in a barn. His cousin was beheaded shortly after his ministry began. He never owned his own home. His life and safety were threatened throughout his ministry. He was hated by a lot of important people. He was rejected by many of his own countrymen. He was going to be deserted by his best friends at his biggest point of need. He was going to be judged unfairly. He was going to be mocked. He was going to be spat upon. He was going to be beaten. He was going to have a crown of thorns rammed onto his head. He was going to carry a cross through Jerusalem and in front of people who once cheered for him.

He was going to be nailed to a cross, and he was going to die for people who didn't seem to care, and still he said to his disciples on the last night of his life—what I previously quoted, but now let me show you the rest of what he said—"I have said these things to you, that in me you may have peace. In the world you will have tribulation. But take heart; *I have overcome the world*" (John 16:33, emphasis added).

Jesus was going to be victimized, but he refused to be a victim.

And so did the first Christians.

Luke paints a picture of a group of believers who were rejoicing, not because they didn't have needs, but because they weren't alone in their loss. They had big needs that could only be met with Christians coming together and selling their "possessions and belongings." And they were rejoicing, not because they weren't suffering, but because they weren't suffering alone.

Jesus suffered too, and he didn't ask, "Why me?"

Satan, the professional killjoy, wants to kill our joy by convincing us that we deserve to be treated better (by God) and that the trials we're enduring are "not fair." Satan loves when people who have been victimized begin to define themselves by their trials. He rejoices when Christians, who have been dealt a bad hand, start to play the victim card. This is what he tried to do in the life of tennis star Arthur Ashe.

Arthur Ashe was one of the most successful professional tennis players of all time. In his career he won three Grand Slam titles and was the first African-American to be selected to the United States Davis Cup tennis team and the only African-American man to win the singles title at Wimbledon, the U.S. Open, and the Australian Open. In the early 1980s, Ashe contracted HIV from a blood transfusion during heart surgery. When this tragedy hit Ashe, he didn't turn his eyes toward himself and start playing the victim. No, he turned his eyes toward God.

I read that Ashe was once asked, "Why does God have to select you for such a bad disease?" To this Ashe replied, "The world over—50 million children start playing tennis, 5 million learn to play tennis, 500,000 learn professional tennis, 50,000 come to the circuit, 5,000 reach the grand slam, 50 reach Wimbledon, 4 to semi final, 2 to the finals, when I was holding a cup I never asked God, 'Why me?' And today in pain I should not be asking God, 'Why me?'"[53]

"Why me?" is like a chambered shell in Satan's shotgun.

Don't be surprised when he aims his weapon in your direction.

We will suffer.

The rain will fall.

The waters will rise.

The flood will come.

And trust me, Devotee, you will be better because of it.

James, the brother of Christ, starts his letter to the church with this teaching, "Count it all joy, my brothers, when you meet trials of various kinds" (James 1:2).

You are going to suffer.

Count it all joy . . . to suffer?

What ya talkin' bout, Willis[54] . . . I mean, James?

Maybe James never had a bad day.

Have you ever had a bad day? My friend, Bob Smiley, is a Christian comedian and a frequent flier. A few years ago, he told me a story about something that happened on a flight he was on.

During the flight, while sitting in his assigned seat, something started dripping on him from the overhead bin. He got the flight attendant's attention and said, "There's something coffee-ish dripping all over me."

The flight attendant looked and surmised, "I don't think it's coffee."

To which Bob replied, "I don't care what it is! I don't want it dripping on me. This is an airplane, not a water ride!" The flight attendant opened the bin to find the source of the leaking and discovered a wet bag.

The flight attendant then asked the passengers, "Whose is this?"

The lady in the seat in front of Bob answered, "That's mine."

The flight attendant said, "Do you have any liquids in your bag?"

The lady replied, "I've got a bag of breast milk in there that may have ruptured."

Have you ever had a bad day?

You will.

James did.

James, the brother of Jesus and author of the New Testament book bearing his name, was also a key leader in the church in Jerusalem. The Jewish historian Josephus records that James was stoned to death.[55] Eusebius, the "father of church history," adds more details.

Now, I must say that some scholars consider Eusebius's account full of legend, but according to Eusebius, James was approached by the scribes and Pharisees for help in squelching the idea that Jesus was the Christ, the Son of the living God. Bad idea.

The scribes and Pharisees believed that Jesus was leading people astray. They then asked James to stand on the "summit of the temple" and tell what they had ordered him to do. Instead he boldly testified that Christ "Himself sitteth in heaven, at the right hand of the Great Power, and shall come on the clouds of heaven."

Once again, according to Eusebius, the scribes and the Pharisees, enraged by his insubordination, threw him off his perch on the temple and began to stone him (he was not killed by the fall) while he began to pray, "I beseech Thee, Lord God our Father, forgive them; for they know not what they do." Then a man with a club hit James in the head, killing him where he prayed.[56]

Regardless of which account you believe, they both end with James being killed for his faith in Christ, so the man who wrote "Count it all joy, my brothers, when you meet trials of various kinds" knew what it was like to have a bad day.

We are going to suffer.

Suffering is one of the consequences of life—and a gift from God that breaks our allegiance to this world and makes us long for heaven.

Remember, Jesus warned us, "In the world you will have tribulation" (John 16:33).

Paul warned us, too, "For it has been granted to you that for the sake of Christ you should not only believe in him but also suffer for his sake" (Philippians 1:29).

Suffering, even "granted" suffering, is no excuse to be unjoyful.

To persecuted Christians.

To suffering saints.

To any Christian who is stuck in traffic, or a bad marriage, or a bad job, Paul says, "Rejoice in the Lord always"

(Philippians 4:4). And then he repeats it for emphasis: "Rejoice."

God is good even when your day is bad. Rejoice!

God is faithful even when your spouse is not. Rejoice!

God is strong even when your body is weak. Rejoice!

God is kind even when hate is all you feel. Rejoice!

God is merciful even when you feel condemned. Rejoice!

God is still on his throne (see Psalm 11:4) even though you feel like your world is off its rocker. Rejoice!

God is still God . . . even if there is something dripping on you from the luggage bin above. Rejoice!

God is still God, even when you are chest deep in a flood. Rejoice!

*   *   *

I love Sunday night services at Journey, and last Sunday night was especially meaningful because that night, joy walked in and sat on the back row of church.

The flood caught many people off guard and left them stranded on roofs and surrounded by rushing, deep, muddy water. People like LaDean and Bob.

At the end of my message last Sunday, I asked for flood victims to raise their hands so we could pray over them. LaDean and Bob, who were seated on the last row, raised their hands. We prayed over them, and the service continued. I had noticed them during worship because they were especially passionate—hands and voices raised in praise.

After the service, I noticed some commotion from my

staff around LaDean and Bob, and it was only then I noticed that they were soaking wet from the chest down. Their shoes were sloshing with water!

I asked what was going on, and my assistant told me that their home had been flooded and they were trapped. They decided enough was enough and it was time to get out, so they escaped from their house, through waist-deep flood-waters, crawled over a barbed-wire fence, walked to their car that was parked on higher ground, and drove straight to church. They came to church that night with a lot of mixed emotions and expectations.

They were seeking wisdom, guidance, and direction. They had just lost everything to the raging floodwaters. And they wanted to thank God. He had saved their lives.

My team rallied and got them warm showers, clean clothes, hot meals, and some supplies to get them through the next few days.

I can't shake the image of LaDean and Bob praising God exuberantly, knowing now that their worship was saturated from the waist down in sewage-tainted water they had traversed because they wanted to get to church.

Devotee, promise me that you will always love Jesus so much, and be filled with so much joy, that you would be willing to crawl over barbed wire and walk through waist-deep, sewage-tainted water for the opportunity to praise him.

The only regret I have about last Sunday night is that we didn't sing "Oh, How I Love Jesus," because LaDean and Bob's presence at Journey last week was infallible proof that if I had shouted out to them, "Oh, LaDean and Bob, do you love Jesus?" they would have replied joyfully, "Oh, yes, we love Jesus!"

And if I had taken an Instagram of them worshipping on that back row last Sunday night, the caption would have read, "Rejoice!"

CHAPTER 12

PRAISING: SIX NICKELS AND THREE DIMES' WORTH OF WORSHIP

Praising God and having favor with all the
people.—Acts 2:47

I RECEIVED a phone call a few years ago from a friend in Indiana. Her church was divided over worship. The young people were desperate to sing some choruses. The older people refused to sing anything that wasn't in the hymnbook. They sat with crossed arms and closed lips during each chorus. I wanted to tell my friend, "There is nothing new under the sun" (Ecclesiastes 1:9).

Worship has always been a controversial issue. Worship is controversial because it's all about God and all about man at the same time. Worship without God will never satisfy us. Worship without man will never satisfy God.

God wants everything from us, and we want everything

for ourselves—and therein lies the tension that gives birth to the controversy. This is evident from the very first time the word *worship* appears in the Bible (Genesis 22:5). God promised Abram everything: a new purpose (father of many nations), a new name (Abraham), and a new home (Canaan). And in return, God wanted everything from Abraham: his son, Isaac.

After these things God tested Abraham and said to him, "Abraham!" And he said, "Here I am." He said, "Take your son, your only son Isaac, whom you love, and go to the land of Moriah, and offer him there as a burnt offering on one of the mountains of which I shall tell you." So Abraham rose early in the morning, saddled his donkey, and took two of his young men with him, and his son Isaac. And he cut the wood for the burnt offering and arose and went to the place of which God had told him. On the third day Abraham lifted up his eyes and saw the place from afar. Then Abraham said to his young men, "Stay here with the donkey; I and the boy will go over there and worship and come again to you." (Genesis 22:1-5)

Tension.

Test.

Choice.

Worship creates tension between what God wants and what we want, and this creates controversy. But controversy was not evident on the Day of Pentecost.

When the church began on the Day of Pentecost, there were no instruments, no hymnbooks, no screens, no church buildings, and no worship traditions to hinder the worship of resident aliens longing to go home. The first expressions of worship were dynamic and not yet limited by cumbersome human traditions. Acts 2:42-47 is a picture of simplicity in regards to worship:

And they devoted themselves to the apostles' teaching and the fellowship, to the breaking of bread and the prayers. And awe came upon every soul, and many wonders and signs were being done through the apostles. And all who believed were together and had all things in common. And they were selling their possessions and belongings and distributing the proceeds to all, as any had need. And day by day, attending the temple together and breaking bread in their homes, they received their food with glad and generous hearts, praising God and having favor with all the people. And the Lord added to their number day by day those who were being saved.

These first expressions of worship were unplanned, unscripted, and spontaneous gatherings of Christians experiencing their newfound joy in the Lord. As I mentioned in the last chapter, the world was not a Christian world. Sunday was just another day to work, so the Christians realized early that they needed to be good stewards of their brief time together.

But it wasn't long before worship services evolved from the spontaneous worship after Pentecost to orderly gatherings.

Paul, in his first letter to the Corinthians, describes the "order" that God wanted restored in their troubled church (1 Corinthians 14:40). He writes:

What then, brothers? When you come together, each one has a hymn, a lesson, a revelation, a tongue, or an interpretation. Let all things be done for building up. If any speak in a tongue, let there be only two or at most three, and each in turn, and let someone interpret. But if there is no one to interpret, let each of them keep silent in church and speak to himself and to God. Let two or three prophets speak, and let the others weigh what is said. If a revelation is made to another sitting there, let the first be silent. For you can all prophesy one by one, so that all may learn and all be encouraged, and the spirits of prophets are subject to prophets. For God is not a God of confusion but of peace. (14:26-33)

Order in worship became custom. A Roman historian, Pliny, writing about AD 110–120 noted the customs that had arisen and were typical of Christian worship:

[The Christians] . . . were in a habit of meeting on a certain fixed day before it was light, when they sang in alternate verses a hymn to Christ, as to a god, and bound themselves by a solemn oath, not to any wicked deeds, but never to commit any fraud, theft or adultery, never to falsify their word, nor deny a trust when they should be called upon to deliver it up; after which it was their custom to separate, and then reassemble to partake of food—but food of an ordinary and innocent kind.[57]

As time passed, Christian worship gatherings became more organized, and customs grew into traditions. An early church leader, Justin Martyr, writing in about AD 150, describes, in detail, early worship services and some of the traditions that had developed:

> We always remind one another of these things [our
> teachings]. Those who have provide for all those
> in want. We are always together with one another.
> And for all the things with which we are supplied
> we bless the Maker of all through his Son Jesus
> Christ and through his Holy Spirit. And on the day
> called Sunday there is a gathering together in the
> same place of all who live in a city or a rural district.
> The memoirs of the apostles or the writings of the
> prophets are read, as long as time permits. Then
> when the reader ceases, the president in a discourse
> admonishes and urges the imitation of these good
> things. Next we all rise together and send up prayers.
> And, as I said before, when we cease from our
> prayer, bread is presented and wine and water. The
> president in the same manner sends up prayers and
> thanksgivings according to his ability, and the people
> sing out their assent saying the "Amen." A distribution
> and participation of the elements for which thanks

have been given is made to each person, and to those who are not present it is sent by the deacons. Those who have means and are willing, each according to his own choice, gives what he wills, and what is collected is deposited with the president. He provides for the orphans and widows, those who are in want on account of sickness or some other causes, those who are in bonds and strangers who are sojourning, and in a word he becomes the protector of all who are in need. We all make our assembly in common on the day of the Sun, since it is the first day, on which God changed the darkness and matter and made the world, and Jesus Christ our Savior arose from the dead on the same day. For they crucified him on the day before Saturn's day, and on the day after (which is the day of the Sun) he appeared to his apostles and taught his disciples these things.[58]

The first Christ-followers had some powerful and meaningful traditions. Now, I'm not sure if that word *tradition* carries baggage in your mind. I hope not. Traditions aren't bad. Traditions are a normal and healthy part of life. Traditionalism, though, is another matter. Yale historian and theologian Jaroslav Pelikan said, "Tradition is the living faith of the dead, traditionalism is the dead faith of the living."[59] In my opinion, as traditionalism took hold of Christian worship, the tension between what God wants and what we want led Christians to forget the point of worship.

Devotee, I want you to not just love Jesus; I want you also to love to praise Jesus and never forget the point of praise—something that happens more often than it should.

I've done it. I've experienced things in worship services that created tension, tested my patience, and led me to choose to complain to the powers that be, so I understood when a person at church handed me this note recently: "I am no music scholar, but I feel I know appropriate church music when I hear it. Last Sunday's new hymn—if you can call it that—sounded like a sentimental love ballad one would expect to hear crooned in a saloon. If you insist on exposing us to rubbish like this—in God's house!—don't be surprised if many of the faithful look for a new place to worship. The hymns we grew up with are all we need."

Our church has been growing rapidly and holding four services every Sunday in a remodeled movie theater to accommodate the crowds. Our worship services are not what most mainstream Christians would call "traditional," and they haven't been for a while.

This past summer our congregation moved into a new building, which brought a lot of changes. Change is hard and tests traditions. We have kept a lot of our traditions, but we have also embraced some new ones with the hopes of enhancing our corporate praise and reaching lost people in our community for Christ.

During this move we've started singing some new songs and using some new technology. I have received several e-mails and handwritten notes from faithful Journey members expressing their concerns about our worship services. Most of the written comments I've received have been gracious, kind, encouraging, and seasoned with faithful wisdom on the changes we've made and the impact of those changes on certain members in the congregation. A few, similar to the one I quoted above, had a more critical tone and warned that the writers were going to leave the church if the changes continued.

I need to let you know that, although it sounded exactly like a couple of the notes I received this past summer, the note I quoted above wasn't written in 2013; it was written in 1863. And it wasn't referring to a new Hillsong United song; it was referring to the "new" hymn "Just as I Am." [60]

I've been around churches my entire life and I've studied church history, so I know Solomon was right when he wrote, "There is nothing new under the sun" (Ecclesiastes 1:9). Too often, we miss the point of praise and write angry notes to pastors—forgetting that worship is not only about what we want; it's about what God wants.

Do you know what God wants?

Our praise. He actually craves it.

In John 4 we find Jesus interacting with a Samaritan woman at Jacob's well. At this well, Jesus shares a lot of truths to help satisfy her—and our—thirst for what will truly satisfy, and then Jesus tells this woman a final and most astonishing truth: God wants us to worship him. Jesus says, "But the hour is coming, and is now here, when the true worshipers will worship the Father in spirit and truth, for the Father is seeking such people to worship him" (verse 23). The word used here for "seeking" is the Greek word *zeteo*, which is only used nine times in the New Testament. This word means "to crave."

Amazing! God craves our worship.

What do you crave?

I crave movie theater popcorn, so I've purchased a bucket for eighteen dollars that allows me to get refills for only three dollars, and I can fill up every Sunday night on the way home from church for the rest of the year.

God craves our worship, so he purchased our lives with the life of his Son.

Any parent of a child understands this craving. It's what we feel as the words "I love you" flow for the first time from the lips of the children we have cherished since before their birth. God craves this from us.

He craves our love. He craves our praise. Let's give it to him.

Do you know what I mean when I say "praise"? Praise is an expression of thanks and love for God.

THANKS

When children are little, parents often prompt them to express gratitude for someone else's sacrifice by asking, "What do you say?" The children's response is praise. It doesn't have to be fancy; it just has to be heartfelt . . . or at least it should be.

Are you grateful for what God has done for you?

God has done so much for us, and I could start listing all of the reasons we have to say thanks to him. However, there is not enough time or paper on this planet to sufficiently do the job, so let me just give you one reason to say thanks to God: freedom.

When Adam and Eve freely chose to eat that piece of fruit, they enslaved humankind forever in the shackles of sin. But in Christ we are liberated. The apostle Paul says it this way: "There is therefore now no condemnation for those who are in Christ Jesus. For the law of the Spirit of life has set you free in Christ Jesus from the law of sin and death" (Romans 8:1-2).

In Christ, we've been liberated. What do you say?

When the multitudes cried out, "Crucify him!" (Mark 15:13) in opposition to the release of Jesus, they unknowingly enslaved themselves in shackles of guilt. But they realized—through Peter's message—that they could be liberated in Christ. Peter exhorted, "'Save yourselves from this crooked generation.' So those who received his word were baptized, and there were added that day about three thousand souls" (Acts 2:40-41).

And what did they say after their liberation? "And day by day, attending the temple together and breaking bread in their homes, they received their food with glad and generous hearts, *praising God* and having favor with all the people. And the Lord added to their number day by day those who were being saved" (Acts 2:46-47, emphasis added).

The middle-aged lame beggar (see Acts 4:22) was enslaved by the disability of his own legs and essentially shackled in a spot called the "Beautiful Gate of the temple" (Acts 3:10) when Peter and John healed him through the power of God. And what did he say after his liberation? "And leaping up he stood and began to walk, and entered the temple with them, walking and leaping and *praising God*" (Acts 3:8, emphasis added).

Peter and John were enslaved in real shackles (see Acts 4:3), and upon their providential release, do you know what they and their fellow Christians said? "When they were released, they went to their friends and reported what the chief priests and the elders had said to them. And when they heard it, they *lifted their voices together to God*" (Acts 4:23-24, emphasis added).

The apostles were enslaved in shackles of jealously by the high priest and his lynch mob, the Sadducees, because the apostles were healing sick people and casting out unclean spirits. Upon their release, do you know what they said? "Then they left the presence of the council, *rejoicing* that they were counted worthy to suffer dishonor for the name" (Acts 5:41, emphasis added).

Paul and Silas were enslaved in shackles in a Philippian prison for freeing a slave girl from a spirit of divination (see Acts 16:16-18), and while they were still in captivity, do you know what they said? "About midnight Paul and Silas were *praying and singing hymns to God*" (Acts 16:25, emphasis added).

From what bondage has Christ freed you?

Bondage to fear? What do you say?

Bondage to pain? What do you say?

Bondage to anger? What do you say?

Bondage to addiction? What do you say?

Bondage to the wages of sin? What do you say?

Bondage to death? What do you say?

Praise flows freely out of a liberated soul. It shouldn't have to be prompted out of you. It shouldn't be difficult. Just release gratitude God's direction for the fact of your liberation in Christ from the wages of sin and death, and it will be called "praise."

But praise is also an expression of love.

LOVE

I love my wife, a lot, so I tell her.

I write it with a bar of soap on her mirror. I text it to her. I e-mail it to her. I send her Facebook messages documenting it. I call her several times a day to remind her of it. I testify to it in pictures I post of her and us on Instagram. I write it in cards. I tell my congregation of it in my sermons. I say it of her in front of my children. I mention it in books I write. I'd say it in smoke signals if I could find enough wood.

I love my wife, so I say it.

I don't have to work at it; it just flows out of me.

Now, I didn't know Rhonda (my hot wife, whom I love) twenty-six years ago, so I didn't love her then. But after I met her and got to know her . . . respect her . . . like her . . . enjoy being around her . . . I started to love her.

You may have just met Jesus and just started getting to

know him, and you may be a little uncomfortable expressing your love for a nice, bearded Jewish man who wears robes and sandals, teaches really well, died a really horrible and unfair death—and whom you believe is the Son of God . . . and that's okay. But I hope you start to love him.

It's what he wants. It's what he craves. It's what he commands: "You shall love the Lord your God with all your heart and with all your soul and with all your mind. This is the great and first commandment" (Matthew 22:37-38).

As you've read in this book already, it's what he asked of Peter three times, "Do you love me?" (John 21:15-17).

With Allison Scott (my friend's daughter I mentioned earlier who decided to graduate from Ozark Christian College), I want you to get to the point, sooner rather than later, in your relationship with Jesus that you just can't contain it: "I just love Jesus!"

I want you to develop it. I want you to feel it. I want you to nourish it. I want you to cherish it. I want you to acknowledge it, believing that everyone who acknowledges him before men, he will also acknowledge before his Father who is in heaven (see Matthew 10:32). I want you to honk your car horn and let the whole world know it!

Like Buddy the Elf, throw off your furry hat, spin around, and declare, "I'm in love, I'm in love, and I don't care who knows it!" and it will be called "praise."

Praise doesn't need to be planned—just express it spontaneously. Praise doesn't need to be perfect—just express it honestly. Praise doesn't need to be pretentious—just express it simply. Praise shouldn't have to be prompted—it just needs to be expressed lovingly.

Many years ago I got sick. I had a really high fever and—being a guy—thought I was close to death. Unprompted, my daughter Ashton, who was about four years old at the time, came into my room with some coins she wanted to give to me held tightly in her tiny right hand. Rhonda had followed her in and could see the internal struggle she was experiencing, so she put her hand on top of Ashton's blonde head and said, "Sweetie, you don't have to give your money to Daddy."

Tension.

Test.

Choice.

Ashton replied, "I don't really care. I want to give it to Daddy."

"I love you, Ashtie," I said.

"I love you, too, Daddy," she expressed.

And, with those words, she placed her six nickels and three dimes on the nightstand beside my head.

Now, you may call that sacrifice sixty cents, but I call it "praise."

CHAPTER 13

GROWING: THE MAGIC PILL

And the Lord added to their number day by day those who were being saved.—Acts 2:47

NINE YEARS AGO, after the birth of our fourth and last child, my wife and I lamented that we were done having kids. We love our kids and especially enjoy them when they're little, so we were excited when we took our new daughter, Payton, to the doctor for the first time and he told us about an astonishing medical discovery that could change our lives.

He told us about a new pill that had just been approved for use by the FDA. He called it the *Magic Pill*. It's a pill that, when given to our daughter, would stop her growth.

My wife and I thought about the possibilities for a while. . . .

First, Payton would never change. No need for child

safety latches. No terrible twos. No potty training. She'd never have to face the unpleasant experience of being picked last for kickball at school. We wouldn't have to watch her go through her awkward teen years when crooked teeth, zits, and glasses would spoil the perfect face we currently enjoyed. She wouldn't ever be burdened with the arduous choice of a college, a career, or a mate. If she never changed, then she'd always be our little girl. No changes—no surprises—for the rest of her life and ours.

Second, Payton would also be less expensive if she remained a month old for the rest of her life. It's a big investment to raise a child from birth to adulthood. Sure, diapers are expensive, but not as expensive as back-to-school clothes, pink bikes with multicolored tassels dangling from the grips of the handlebars, braces, a prom dress, graduation presents, college, a car, a wedding, and a house. If Payton never grew up, then just think of how much money we could save! You don't have to think about it; I know. It's going to cost us $372,934 to raise Payton until the age of eighteen.[61]

And finally, as we considered this *Magic Pill*, we realized that giving Payton this pill would guarantee that she'd be less apt to get hurt. It's safer to keep her as an infant. She'd never roll, crawl, walk, ride, skip, run, drive, or fly away, so she'd never risk injury or stray too far from those who love her best. She'd stay put . . . and that would give us peace of mind. She'd never get hurt . . . and that would save us untold stress. When babies are allowed to grow, they sometimes make foolish choices. My wife can testify that when our daughter was a month old, she never made a foolish choice. In fact, as far as we can tell—she'd never made a choice at all. The *Magic Pill* would guarantee that Payton would never do anything to disappoint us, oppose us, or hurt us or herself. She'd always be safe. She'd do exactly what we wanted her to do and be exactly where we wanted her to be: safe . . . forever.

Obviously, I'm being facetious, but, if there really were a *Magic Pill*, would your church take one? Would you?

The early church was growing explosively. It started growing on the very first day. Peter preached, and the church grew immediately, when three thousand people received the gospel and were baptized (see Acts 2:41). And it kept growing, every day. Luke tells us, "And the Lord added to their number day by day those who were being saved" (Acts 2:47). By the time we get to Acts 4:4, the church in Jerusalem was now running about five thousand men—not counting women (a cultural thing back then).

The growth was uncontainable. We read in Acts 5, "And more than ever believers were added to the Lord, multitudes of both men and women" (verse 14). The church was growing so rapidly that even Jewish priests—who you would think would be incredibly hard to convert because they are not just Jewish, but teachers of Judaism—were coming to Christ. Luke records, "And the word of God continued to increase, and the number of the disciples multiplied greatly in Jerusalem, and a great many of the priests became obedient to the faith" (Acts 6:7).

Regular Christians and the apostles were preaching every

day and everywhere they went, and "the churches were strengthened in the faith, and they increased in numbers daily" (Acts 16:5).

Healthy things grow—it's God's divine plan—and the church was growing because it was a healthy body made up of healthy people. God's ultimate plan is for healthy babies to grow into healthy adults who believe in him, love him, serve him, and tell others about him so that all people can spend eternity with him. God has the same plan for you, his Devotee.

In my life I have had the privilege of worshipping with hundreds of churches and with hundreds of thousands of other Christians around the world . . . and I have come to a conclusion: I think that some people would like to take a *Magic Pill* and give one to their church. They would prefer their church to be small, and they would prefer to remain spiritual infants.

Let me deal with the church side of this for a moment.

Only two percent of churches in America attract more than one thousand adults in a typical weekend. However, these churches—and their dynamic leaders—attract almost one hundred percent of the attention of Christian media, so it might be easy to forget that most of the Protestant churches in America are actually small. George Barna found that the typical Protestant church has eighty-nine adults in attendance during a typical weekend.[62]

A few summers ago my wife and I were driving on I-90 in New York, and we saw a sign at exit 33 advertising the

"World's Smallest Church." It seats two people. It's non-denominational and accessible only by boat. (That's vision for you.)

Maybe the church you attend is proud of its smallness, maybe not.

Regardless, small churches are important and valuable to the kingdom. In my experience, many small churches are full of, and produce, spiritual giants. Many are healthy and growing but will never have more than one hundred people on any Sunday for many reasons that are beyond their control—not the least of which is being located in a remote area surrounded by few residents. I agree with George Barna when he reminds us that "Jesus did not die on the cross to fill up church auditoriums. He died so that people might know God personally and be transformed in all dimensions of their life through their ongoing relationship with Him. Such a personal reformation can happen in a church of any size. After all, the goal of every church should not be numerical growth but spiritual health and vitality."[63]

Which brings me to what I really want to talk about.

You—not the church you attend—because I want the same thing for you: spiritual health and vitality.

Devotee, as you begin your relationship with Christ, resolve now to be a healthy and vital disciple of Christ. Reject the *Magic Pill*! If some well-meaning Christ-follower fills out a prescription so you can get your own bottle of *Magic Pills*, tear it up. If you've already taken one, spit it out. If someone offers you a *Magic Pill* out behind the church building from the trunk of his or her car before the service next Sunday morning, just say no. If your pastor promotes the use of the *Magic Pill* and drives a car with a "If You're Looking for a Church Who Still Believes in the *Magic Pill*... Follow Me!" bumper sticker, run away.

You are a new creation in Christ. The "old" you is gone. When you gave your life to Jesus, you were born again. You were born, like an infant is born, and infants are supposed to grow. They're not supposed to remain infants forever.

Just ask Martilee Covington's mom.

Vanessa Covington had dreams for her daughter, Martilee—dreams she expressed in a short story posted on her blog. In her post Vanessa wrote:

> In the corner of my daughter's room sits a child-size
> wicker chair. Not quite blue. Not quite lavender.
> I bought it for Martilee's first birthday with
> anticipation of tea parties, teddy bears and dress-up
> bonnets. I dreamed of special mommy-daughter
> times—escapes from the world of her two older
> brothers and bugs, balls and guns made of sticks.
> I knew it would be a while before she was actually
> old enough to sip juice from a miniature tea cup and
> make-believe her bear was a royal guest. Until then
> the chair could sit in her room; a throne awaiting its
> princess.
>
> Shortly after her first birthday my little girl's life
> became filled with doctors, blood tests, EEGs and

more doctors. Instead of dreaming of tea parties
I wondered why she could no longer hold her sippy
cup. Instead of anticipating her saying, "I love
you, Mommy," I questioned why she had stopped
babbling. How would she ever run into my arms for
a hug when her legs couldn't hold up her tiny body?
How would she play make-believe when reality was
she may have a terminal illness?

While still searching for answers, our family
prepared to move to another state. Gathering up
things to sell on a yard sale before the big move,
I pondered that little wicker chair that was never
quite the right color to match the room. Maybe
I should just sell it. After all, my tea party dreams
seemed to be fading right before my eyes. [64]

After a year's worth of testing and endless questions, the Covingtons were told that Martilee has Rett syndrome, a neurological disorder that affects speech, hand skills, and coordination. It can also include seizures, irregular breathing, curvature of the spine, and a myriad of other symptoms. Rett syndrome robs her of the ability to walk or talk because it slows down growth and reverses development. To this day, Martilee remains locked in her own body—trapped in the world of infancy. But praise God the story doesn't end there.

Vanessa also wrote, "There have been some rough times and I have shed lots of tears. But I didn't sell that little wicker chair before we moved. It is in Martilee's new room now. . . .

I haven't given up on those tea party dreams."[65]

Tea-party dreams . . . filled with hope.

It would be tragic for you to remain a spiritual infant—for you to never grow in your relationship with Jesus as a disciple of Jesus. Jesus has dreams for your life too, and just like Vanessa and her daughter, God won't give up on his dreams for you to grow either. Don't let where you are in life be the end of your story. Be on guard for the following three reasons most often given for swallowing that aforementioned pill.

CHANGE IS BAD

Sameness is comforting.

I like entering a McDonald's in Omaha, Nebraska, ordering a Big Mac, and knowing that it's going to taste the same as it does back in Greeley, Colorado.

I wrote most of this book at the high table shaped like a pickle that stands against the back wall of the Blue Mug Coffee Bar. I started every writing session listening to "Skyfall" by Adele. I prayed every time I sat down to write this book. This evening, I'm going to be sitting down to work with the same editor I've worked with for every book I've written. Every day, during the course of writing this book, I wore the same pair of socks . . . just kidding!

I get sameness.

I do sameness.

But I also know that sameness can be devastating, especially when it comes to spiritual maturity. God expects us to grow. Through Paul, he says it this way:

And he gave the apostles, the prophets, the evangelists, the shepherds and teachers, to equip the saints for the work of ministry, for building up the body of Christ, until we all attain to the unity of the faith and of the knowledge of the Son of God, to mature manhood, to the measure of the stature of the fullness of Christ, so that we may no longer be children, tossed to and fro by the waves and carried about by every wind of doctrine, by human cunning, by craftiness in deceitful schemes. Rather, speaking the truth in love, we are to grow up in every way into him who is the head, into Christ. (Ephesians 4:11-15)

We are supposed to grow up in every way, and that means change. No *Magic Pills* in Paul's prescription.

Change is life.

Life is change.

Change is scary to people who cherish sameness, so sometimes they will passively—or aggressively—resist change. Christians who don't like change refuse to give up their seats for a first-time guest, their old building for a new building, and their preferences in music styles. Instead they fight, afraid that if they give an inch on the use of hymnbooks, they'll be dragged a mile closer to hell by some pierced teenager with a loud electric guitar, a video projector, and an ungodly agenda.

But God designed this world and everything in it to change. Day to night, winter to spring, and birth to death are all essential cycles in a healthy life. In God's design for your life, you will grow; you will change into a more mature Christ-follower every day.

Embrace change.

Celebrate change.

IT WILL COST YOU

I can still see her standing on the end of that diving board, water dripping off her body, knees shaking, and evoking the words—or, at least, her version of the words—of one of her favorite movies at that time, *Anastasia*, to muster the courage to jump: "Heart, don't fail me now. Courage don't deserve ("deserve" was her word, but the real word was "desert") me!"

There's a cost to jumping.

Ashton knew that, which is why she was singing for courage.

Ashton, my oldest daughter, is in college now, so—as the one who is helping to pay her tuition—let me testify right here and now that change is expensive. She didn't have college tuition when she was an infant, and the most expensive things we purchased for her at that stage were diapers. But she also didn't talk to me, run from across the room and jump into my arms, write me cute texts, buy me nice Christmas gifts, sing me my favorite songs, and fall in love with a really good young man whom she's marrying in a month. (Which is costing me a lot of money. And by "a lot of money," I mean "A LOT of money.") But I'm willing to pay the price for her growth. "Heart, don't fail *me* now!"

Yes, there is a price to pay for change. I hope you are willing to pay the price of following Jesus to wherever he may lead you to do whatever he wants you to do.

What does it cost to follow Jesus? Jesus quantified it this way: "If anyone would come after me, let him deny himself and take up his cross daily and follow me" (Luke 9:23).

There are three things I know for sure about the cross Christ asks you to carry.

First, taking up his cross will change you forever.

Second, taking up his cross will cost you everything.

And third, taking up the cross of Christ brings rewards that are out of this world!

IT'S NOT SAFE

As you grow in your relationship with Christ and as his disciple, I want you to promise me that you won't play it safe. I don't want you to have a safing faith.

No, I'm not an idiot. I meant to write "safing faith," not "saving faith." *Safing faith* is a phrase I invented to define the attempt by some churches and Christians to make faith safe. I believe in saving faith, but I am opposed to any human attempts to make faith in God *safe*.

There is a famous scene in *The Lion, the Witch and the Wardrobe* by C. S. Lewis in which Lucy learns that Aslan, the king they are waiting for, is, in fact, a full-grown lion. She asks if he is safe, to which Mr. Beaver replies, "Safe? . . . Who said anything about safe? 'Course he isn't safe. But he's good."[66]

God is definitely good, but he is not safe. In Deuteronomy 4:24 we read, "For the Lord your God is a consuming fire, a jealous God."

A consuming fire is not safe. A consuming fire is not controllable. A consuming fire is not manageable. A consuming fire is not predictable. A consuming fire must be respected. A consuming fire does not submit to our plans. It does not stop. It does not fade away. It takes what it wants and leaves when it is finished. It cannot be put out with our words, our opinions, our criticisms, or be extinguished with the waving of our bulletins containing our well-planned worship services.

God—*the* consuming fire—will not be contained. He is powerful, and our attempts to make our church services and spiritual lives safe are laughable.

I don't want to be safe! I want to be faithful. I want to build an ark, lay my all on the altar, tell Pharaoh what to do, walk around the walled city, face the giant, square off against the prophets of Baal, get out of the boat, and even stand face-to-face with a hungry lion if that's what God calls me to do. I don't want a safing faith; I want a saving faith.

As far as I'm concerned, safing faith is for wimps!

Here's what a safing faith looks like in Christians:

- Never sharing your faith
- Having no non-Christian friends
- Never singing too loud
- Never opening up to other Christians

- Never praying in public
- Sitting in the boat when given the chance to tread the waves
- Giving only ten percent
- Never crying in front of your church or small group
- Never expressing doubts
- Never opening a Bible in private
- Never carrying a Bible in public
- Never evangelizing—building an intentional relationship through which someone can be introduced to Jesus Christ
- Praying sporadically and only for wants
- Sitting while singing "The Stand" by Hillsong United
- Tolerating a lack of ethnic diversity in your church
- Criticizing the preacher when his message makes you uncomfortable
- Criticizing me for expecting too much of you
- Having an obsession with your personal comfort
- Going to church instead of being the church
- Making fun of homosexuals instead of eating with them
- Not clapping after a baptism
- Criticizing enthusiastic faith in young people and new converts
- Never going on a mission trip
- Talking about what God can do and what you'll do for God, but then doing nothing when God gives you the opportunity to do something for him

- Getting fear-induced paralysis in moments requiring a step of faith
- Selling the wicker chair in a yard sale and giving up on tea-party dreams

And, here's what a safing faith looks like in churches:

- Plenty of available seating and parking spaces
- Passion for the bylaws
- Long board meetings and short prayer meetings
- No prayer at leadership meetings and no leaders at prayer meetings
- All steps of faith approved by a congregational vote of at least 70 percent
- Saving seats preferred to saving souls
- Expectation that the preacher will do all of the evangelism since that's "what he's paid to do"
- Toleration of cliques
- Abundance of selfishness
- Unhealthy and unrealistic veneration of the past
- Obsession with keeping on schedule and finishing on time
- Fixation on corporate comfort
- No support for world evangelism
- An unusually large Policies and Procedures manual
- No, or very little, missions effort
- Budget-driven vision, not vice versa

- Bold moves only when there's enough money in the bank to pay for it
- Fear-induced paralysis in moments requiring a step of faith
- And a large bottle of *Magic Pills* in the foyer

If there were such thing as a *Magic Pill* that keeps people from growing, my wife and I would refuse to give it or take it—and I hope you would too, because life is about growth and growth is about life.

Life here.

Life later.

Life eternal.

Devotee, it's all about salvation.

It was for the first Christians. When, through Peter's presentation of the gospel, they realized they were lost, they cried out, "Brothers, what shall we do?" (Acts 2:37).

It was for Peter on Pentecost, so he exhorted, "Save yourselves from this crooked generation" (Acts 2:40).

It is for the Lord, so he grew his church: "And the Lord added to their number day by day those who were being saved" (Acts 2:47).

And he'll help you to grow too.

Just wait upon him. Trust in him. See him for who he really is.

Speak about him to anyone who will listen. Learn about him. Share life with other Devotees.

Remember the sacrifices he made for you. Communicate

with him through prayer. Believe in him and what he can do in and through you. Sacrifice whatever he tells you to sacrifice.

Enjoy the life he's given you. Praise him. Grow and resolve to keep growing up in him.

And move out to the edge of the board and sing, if you must.

No matter what, Devotee, remember the key to developing your relationship with Jesus, as his disciple, can be found in Peter's answer to Christ's question, "Do you love me?"

"Yes, Lord; you know that I love you" (John 21:16).

It's love. It's all about love, always has been and always will be.

This is the key to developing your relationship with Jesus as his disciple: Devoted love. Nothing more; nothing less.

It's not about religion; it's about a relationship with Jesus. It's not about obligation to Christ; it's about affection for Christ. It's not about following a plan; it's about falling more in love with Jesus. It's not about duty; it's about devotion. It's not just about confessing our faith; it's also about confessing our love. It's not just about following his teachings; it's about fanatically following him.

And it's not about leading new converts through "Ten Simple Steps for Becoming a Better Disciple"; it's about being a Devotee to Christ who explains each step of faith by boldly proclaiming, "I just love Jesus!"

Just love.

THE 40-DAY DEVOTED EXPERIENCE

—————

RECENTLY, a friend of mine spoke about a time when he and his family were at the beach. His daughter Sara was afraid to get into the water. Knowing how much fun she would have, he coaxed her, saying, "Sara, just put your toes in." Reluctantly, she did and then exclaimed as the water rushed through her tiny toes, "It feels funny!" My friend smiled and said, "That's the water loving you."

Next thing he knew, Sara was moving deeper and deeper until she was fully immersed in the water—and having the time of her life!

When you gave your life to Jesus Christ, you entered into a relationship with him. I wrote this book with the hope that—as you begin or rekindle your relationship with Jesus— you'll refuse to just stick your toes in the water. Decide now that, in your relationship with Jesus, you're going to jump in and go deeper into his love for you and your love for him. I promise you that if you do, you'll have the time of your life!

This guide is designed to facilitate a 40-Day experience

through which you fall more in love with Jesus. As I describe in chapter 1, allow the Holy Spirit to lead you through this experience. *Devoted* is written to also serve as a sort of theological primer—leading you through some key theological issues.

Don't rush through this 40-Day experience. I want this to be like a honeymoon period in your relationship with Jesus.

Get to know him. Talk with him. Listen to him. Wait upon the Lord to lead you wherever it is he wants to take you.

Just follow.

Just trust.

Just wait.

Just love.

If this experience begins to feel like work, take a break. Remember, what I'm going to lead you through is not about following a plan; it's about falling more in love with Jesus.

So let's begin. I hope you have the time of your life!

DAY ONE: (This plan is designed to be started on a Monday.) Often, our conversion to Christ is an emotional experience. Like the first Christ-followers on the Day of Pentecost, we feel convicted of our sin, and with a "What shall we do?" (Acts 2:37) in our hearts, we rush to the altar, pray a prayer, make a confession, and allow ourselves to be immersed in the baptistery, only to then wonder, "What have I done?"

Today, as we begin this 40-Day experience, I want you to remember the day you began your relationship with Jesus. Write down as many details as you can remember—date, location, circumstances, people who were used by God to bring you to the point of conversion, and especially the reasons you felt led to give your life to Christ. Down the road, when you wonder, "What have I done?" this will help you remember.

My Testimony:

_____

_____

_____

_____

Close your time with Jesus by finishing this prayer: "Lord, thanks for what you've done in my life . . ."

DAY TWO:

Read "A Word Before."

When you hear the word *disciple*, what images come to mind?

Write your own definition for *disciple* here:

_____

When you hear the word *Devotee*, what images come to mind?

List a few of the things to which you've been devoted in your life:

_____

_____

How have these devotions impacted your life? Positively? Negatively?

_____

_____

_____

Close your time with Jesus by finishing this prayer: "Lord, I want to be fanatically devoted to you . . . "

DAY THREE:

Read "Introduction: Just Love."

When was the first time you fell in love?

How did you know you were in love?

When was the first time you felt loved?

How did you know you were loved?

List a few of the most important questions you've been asked in your life:

_____

_____

_____

_____

Now, after each question, share how your answer to each question impacted your life.

Close your time with Jesus by finishing this prayer: "Lord, I want to love you more . . ."

DAY FOUR:

Throughout today list all of the reasons why you love Jesus.

Why I Love You, Jesus:

Close your time with Jesus by finishing this prayer: "Lord, I love you . . ."

_____

_____

_____

_____

DAY FIVE:

Read chapter 1, "Waiting: True Love Waits," today.

When do you have the hardest time being patient? Why?

When did you have to wait for something and it was worth it? Not worth it?

Close your time with Jesus by offering this prayer: "Lord, I'm listening. What do you want me to hear?"

DAY SIX:

Today, I want you to carry around a blank notepad or piece of paper with this heading: **"Lord, I'm listening . . ."**

Pray this prayer throughout the day: "Lord, I'm listening. What do you want me to hear?"

During the day, write down anything you think the Lord might be trying to say to you.

DAY SEVEN:

Read Psalm 46:10.

Today, focus on being as still as possible—in your words, with your actions, with your bodily movements, with your thoughts, and with your plans.

Pray this prayer in quiet moments today: "Lord, help me to remain still and not move until you move me."

DAY EIGHT:

Read chapter 2, "Trusting: Of Dependency and Dynamite," today.

Start listing the things you trust in. List as many as you can think of.

Things I Trust:

_____

_____

_____

_____

When you are done, think about your life and the choices you make. Based on how you live your life, circle the top five things in which you trust the most.

Close your time with Jesus by finishing this prayer: "Lord, I want to trust you . . ."

DAY NINE:

Today, I want you to list your greatest fears.

My Greatest Fears:

_____

_____

_____

_____

When your list is complete, pray this prayer over each fear: "Lord, please replace this fear with faith."

DAY TEN:

Today, you're going to do something for the Lord that requires faith—a "Catch me, Dad" act.

Before doing anything, pray this prayer: "Lord, I want to trust you more. Today, I want to take a step of faith. Help me to know what that step of faith is and then to have the courage to take it."

After you take your step of faith, fill this out: *With faith in God, on this date:* _____ , *I* _____

_____.

DAY ELEVEN:

Read chapter 3, "Seeing: Love at First Sight," today.

Write a description of Jesus, as if you were describing him to someone who has never heard of him.

Let Me Introduce You to Jesus:

_____

_____

_____

_____

Close your time with Jesus by finishing this prayer: "Lord, I want to see you more . . ."

DAY TWELVE:

Today, I want you to list all of the ways you see the Lord. Carry a notepad or a piece of paper with you and—throughout the day—write down anything through which you see the Lord more clearly.

If you have the ability with your cell phone or with a camera, take pictures of things that help you to see the Lord more clearly and—if you'd like—upload them on the _Devoted_ book Facebook page (https://www.facebook.com/devoteddiscipleship) so others can see the Lord more clearly too.

DAY THIRTEEN:

Read chapter 4, "Speaking: To Tell the Truth."

In his book *Abba's Child,* Brennan Manning writes, "Silent solitude makes true speech possible and personal. If I am not in touch with my own belovedness, then I cannot touch the sacredness of others. If I am estranged from myself, I am likewise a stranger to others."[67]

With this in mind—as much as your life, schedule, and family will allow—spend the rest of the day in silence before the Lord.

DAY FOURTEEN:

Since you've been silent for a period of time now, make the first word you utter today a word of praise to the Lord. You may want to write it here: *Lord, I praise you for* _____
_____.

Throughout the rest of the day, speak out as many praises as come to your mind.

Close your day by finishing this prayer: "Lord, my words belong to you . . ."

DAY FIFTEEN:

As a huge proponent of eating with sinners, I've had many occasions where the only "paper" upon which I could write— during a meal, or over a cup of coffee—to help me present the gospel message was a napkin. Over the years, I've learned that I'm not the first person to use this approach. On the Internet, there are several resources that can teach you how to share the gospel on a napkin.

Today, since you just read about the gospel in this book, I want you to develop your own napkin presentation of the gospel. (You can find samples on www.devotedbook.com.)

Just get a napkin or two and start drawing a picture that can help to explain the gospel to someone who does not know Jesus Christ. When you are done, you can upload a picture of your "gospel napkin" on the *Devoted* book Facebook page.

DAY SIXTEEN:
Read chapter 5, "Learning: 'A Mind Is a Terrible Thing to Waste.'"

Write your favorite Bible verse here:

_____

_____

Now memorize it.

Before the end of the day, write it here from memory:

_____

_____

Close your time with Jesus by finishing this prayer: "Lord, I've just hidden your word in my heart . . ."

DAY SEVENTEEN:
What do you believe?

First Corinthians 15:3-11 contains the core beliefs of the first Christ-followers. Take a moment and read that passage. Now, I want you to list your core beliefs about God, Jesus, the Holy Spirit, the Bible, salvation, sin, and so on. It doesn't have to be fancy, or in any particular order; it just has to be a list of what you believe.

What I Believe:

_____

_____

DAY EIGHTEEN:
Read chapter 6, "Sharing: On Pound Cake–Filled Purses."

List the names of your closest Christian friends.

List of My Christian Friends:

_____

_____

_____

_____

Now go back over the list and, to the right of each name, write a word that best describes why you are grateful for him or her.

Go over the list again and pray for each person by name.

DAY NINETEEN:

If you haven't already, watch the "Battle at Kruger" video on YouTube.[68]

List any similarities you see between how those lions attacked that baby water buffalo and how Satan attacks you.

_____

_____

_____

_____

Where are you most vulnerable to an attack from Satan?

What can you do today to better protect yourself from a satanic attack?

Close your time with Jesus by finishing this prayer: "Lord, I know you have defeated Satan . . ."

DAY TWENTY:

List the names of many of your Christian friends and the churches they attend.

My Friends and Their Churches:

_____

_____

_____

_____

_____

Now, pray over your list.

Go to your church's website and find the "Staff" page.

Pray for the staff of your church.

Are you currently in a small group at your church? If so, pray for your group members by name. If not, pray this prayer: "Lord, please lead me to a small group where I can be blessed through fellowship."

DAY TWENTY-ONE:

Read chapter 7, "Remembering: The Descanso at Mile Marker 38."

Stop and remember the death, burial, and resurrection of Jesus Christ through Communion today.

If your church doesn't offer weekly Communion, find a cracker and some grape juice, and have your own time of remembrance. Or better yet, get together with other Christians for an impromptu time of rest and remembrance.

DAY TWENTY-TWO:

I want you to make a real descanso—a cross or emblem that will help you to remember the death, burial, and resurrection of Jesus Christ. You can Google the term *descanso*—looking for images—and you'll find plenty of examples. It doesn't have to be complicated. Just make a simple symbol that you can place somewhere in your home, office, car, yard, or wherever you need to be reminded of what Jesus Christ has done for us.

Close your day by finishing this prayer: "Lord, I thank you for sending Jesus to die on a cross for our sins . . ."

DAY TWENTY-THREE:

Read chapter 8, "Praying: 'I Pledge Allegiance.'"

Take a moment and identify some of the barriers you regularly have to overcome to pray.

Barriers to Prayer:

_____

_____

_____

Now, pray over this list, asking God to remove these barriers.

Close your time with Jesus by praying for as long as possible. Don't rush it. Don't cut it off early. Just start a conversation with God and let him take it wherever he wants it to go.

DAY TWENTY-FOUR:

Today, I want you to try to practice what the apostle Paul preached: "Pray without ceasing" (1 Thessalonians 5:17). This doesn't mean I want you on your knees next to your bed with your hands folded and your eyes closed all day, unless that's what God leads you to do.

No, here's what I want you to do. Early today, begin a conversation with God and just keep it going all day long. There will be gaps in the conversation as you fulfill your other daily responsibilities, but keep coming back to the conversation. Think of it like you have your phone next to you all day with God on speaker.

Close this day with Jesus with a simple, "In Jesus' name, amen."

DAY TWENTY-FIVE:

Read chapter 9, "Believing: Leap!"

List the five biggest challenges you are currently facing.

Challenges:

_____

_____

_____

_____

_____

Now, draw a line through each challenge as you pray this prayer: "Lord, I believe you will help me overcome this challenge."

DAY TWENTY-SIX:
Read Ephesians 3:20.

I want you to ask God for at least five things, and according to the verse you just read, it's okay to dream a little.

Dreams:

_____

_____

_____

_____

Close with this prayer: "Lord, I submit my dreams to your will, but in faith I want to ask you for . . . ."

DAY TWENTY-SEVEN:
Throughout the day, pray this prayer: "Lord, I want to do something for you that will fail unless you're in it."

Before you go to bed tonight, if God lays something on your heart, finish this sentence: *I believe God wants me to* _____

_____

_____.

This cannot be rushed or forced, so if the Lord hasn't revealed anything to you, wait until he does. And, when he does, fill in the blank above.

DAY TWENTY-EIGHT:

Read chapter 10, "Sacrificing: 'Or, Buy Myself a Car!'"

If you had to give up something today for Jesus, what would be the hardest thing to sacrifice?

Sacrifice something for Jesus today.

Close your time with Jesus by finishing this prayer: "Lord, everything belongs to you; even so, today I promise to give you . . ."

DAY TWENTY-NINE:

Reread Philippians 2:3-8.

List the things Jesus sacrificed for us.

Things Jesus Sacrificed:

_____

_____

What one thing are you willing to sacrifice to him today?

Close your time with Jesus by finishing this prayer: "Lord, because I love you, I will give up . . ."

DAY THIRTY:

Make a sacrifice of your time, energy, or money today and then fill this out: *Today I sacrificed* _____ _____ *because I love Jesus.*

DAY THIRTY-ONE:

Read chapter 11, "Enjoying: Waist-Deep in Unexpected Joy."

List the top ten things in your life that bring you joy.

Sources of Joy:

_____

_____

_____

_____

_____

_____

_____

_____

_____

_____

Now, go back over the list and pray this prayer over each thing: "Lord, thank you for . . ."

DAY THIRTY-TWO:
Read James 1:2-4.

List a few of the trials you are facing right now (or have faced in the past) that are making it hard for you to rejoice:

_____

_____

_____

_____

This may be challenging, but give it a try. Beside each trial listed, write how that trial—with God's help—can help you to mature.

Close this time with Jesus by finishing this prayer: "Lord, help me . . ."

DAY THIRTY-THREE:
Read Philippians 4:4.

Be intentional about rejoicing in the Lord throughout this day.

Write the word *Rejoice* on sticky notes and place them on your bathroom mirror, on your refrigerator door, on the dashboard of your car, in your office cubicle, in your locker at school, and anywhere else you need to be reminded to rejoice.

When you see each note, finish this prayer: "Lord, I will rejoice in you always because you have . . ."

DAY THIRTY-FOUR:

Read chapter 12, "Praising: Six Nickels and Three Dimes' Worth of Worship."

List the top ten things you love about the Lord.

_____

_____

_____

_____

_____

_____

_____

_____

_____

_____

Now, pray over your list, adding this prayer before each thing, "Lord, I praise you for . . ."

DAY THIRTY-FIVE:

Read Psalm 100.

The Lord is good.

List at least one way the Lord has been good to you today.

_____

_____

_____

_____

Now bless his name publically for his goodness by tweeting the praise on Twitter, texting the praise to someone, posting your praise on Facebook, e-mailing someone with your praise, or testifying to his goodness when you're at church today.

DAY THIRTY-SIX:

Sometime today I want you to enter into a time of personal worship to rejoice with the One you love.

Find a quiet and private place, select a few of your favorite worship songs or hymns on your iPod or MP3 player, and get a Bible or Bible app, your journal or blank notebook, and something with which to write.

This is to be a time of joy, so prepare your attitude for this time by finishing this prayer: "Lord, I rejoice in you always because . . ."

Now, press play, worship through singing, pray some more, open your Bible and see what God wants to say to you, write down what you hear him say, pray some more, sing some more, and—no matter what—give him what he craves.

DAY THIRTY-SEVEN:
Read chapter 13, "Growing: The Magic Pill."

List the top three areas of your life in which you would like to see more growth.

Areas in My Life Where I Want to Grow:

_____

_____

_____

Now, pray this prayer over each area: "Lord, help me to grow . . ."

DAY THIRTY-EIGHT:
Find a whiteboard or blank piece of paper and start listing everything you do in a typical week. Next to each activity that promotes spiritual growth, write a *g*. Are you happy with what you see? If not, make some changes.

Now, pray this prayer: "Lord, help me to prioritize my life in a way that honors you and helps me to grow into the person you want me to be."

DAY THIRTY-NINE:
Read John 21:15-19.

Peter denied knowing Jesus three times, but because of the grace of God he was allowed to proclaim his love for Christ three times.

Devotee, I pray that you'll proclaim your love for Christ countless times the rest of your life, but let's start with at least three.

Below, answer each question with a specific reason as to why you love the Lord.

Oh, reader, do you love Jesus?
Oh, yes, I love Jesus, because he _____
_____ .

Oh, reader, do you love Jesus?
Oh, yes, I love Jesus, because he _____
_____ .

Oh, reader, do you love Jesus?
Oh, yes, I love Jesus, because he _____
_____ .

DAY FORTY:

One of the most important parts of a marriage ceremony is when the couple makes vows to each other before God. You are in a relationship with Jesus, and as we finish this 40-Day experience and because you just love Jesus, I want you to take a few moments and write vows to him.

They don't need to be fancy; they just need to be sincere.

My Vows to Jesus:

_____

_____

_____

_____

_____

_____

_____

When your vows are completed, close this 40-Day experience by praying these vows to the One you love: "Jesus, because I just love you, I vow to . . ."

More

Please visit www.devotedbook.com for the following resources:

- The *40-Day Devoted Experience* in pdf.
- Downloadable questions for each chapter of *Devoted* for use in small groups, Sunday school, or individual study.
- A five-week, church-wide program, *Devoted. Devoted* is designed to be used, not just as an individual 40-Day experience, but also in conjunction with a church-wide experience called *Devoted*. On www. devotedbook.com you'll find downloadable sermons, worship plans, small group questions for each chapter, and a variety of resources to help your congregation

experience *Devoted* on a broader level through the 40-Day, church-wide experience, *Devoted*. The following messages are planned to coincide with the 40-Day *Devoted* individual reading experience:

Week One: DEVOTED TO WAITING

Week Two: DEVOTED TO LISTENING

Week Three: DEVOTED TO REMEMBERING

Week Four: DEVOTED TO SACRIFICING

Week Five: DEVOTED TO PRAISING

ACKNOWLEDGMENTS

___

In the introduction to his best-selling book, *Night*, Elie Wiesel wrote, "I believe it important to emphasize how strongly I feel that books, just like people, have a destiny."[69]

I believe the destiny of this book is the raising up and release of a generation of Devotees who are more in love with Jesus every day, and I know that the destiny of this book would still be unrealized if it were not for the love and support of many people.

Let me take a moment and recognize some of them—people whose love and devotion have helped to make this book possible.

Rhonda, my wife—No one knows how much you have to sacrifice every time I embark on writing a book, but I do, and I am profoundly grateful. I'd be a joke without you. I respect you. I cherish you. I adore you. I like you, and . . . yes, I just love you too.

Ashton, Levi, Sylas, and Payton, my children—I can't express how much I love you and how much I love seeing you just love Jesus. I'm so proud to be your dad.

My family: Mom, the Chamberses (thanks for your help with research, Dr. Adam Chambers), the Holbrooks (thanks for opening up your B&B to this weary writer), the Woods, and the Smiths—You are such a blessing to my life. I love you all.

My agent, Blythe Daniel—You are wonderful! Thanks for your ministry to my family and me. I love serving with you.

My trusted friend and writing companion—Twila Sias, I just love you! Thanks for all the time you sacrificed for this book and for teaching me about split infinitives. You are a blessing to me beyond words.

My assistant on this project, Leanne Schaffner (aka, "Dagger Girl")—Little did you know, when you agreed to help me with this project, how much work you'd have to do. Little did I know, when you agreed to help me with this project, how much I would grow to depend on your keen eye, wisdom, and writing abilities. You are gifted, and I'm so grateful for all you did to help me finish this book.

My editor, Jamie Chavez—Your assignment to this project was a gift from God, for which I will always be grateful. I loved working with you—every interaction, every word, every suggestion, every moment. You are amazing! Thanks for sharing your heart, talent, and wisdom with me in such an endearing way. You rock!

My team at NavPress—Meg Wallin, Megan Beam, Rebekah Guzman, Brian Thomasson, Caitlyn Carlson, and Don Pape—Thanks for believing in me, praying over me, for me, and with me, feeding me (at Marigold's), and for ministering alongside me through this book. Being with you was just like being with Jesus. Oh, and that time we prayed with our server, Sherry, was but an earlier heaven.

My friends—Thanks for all you did to help me finish this book. I love you. The Streets, the Davises, the Estrins, the Lightfeet, the Kahlas, the Jenkinses, Darlene Schroeder, the Petersons, the Longs (friends and owners of the Blue Mug—my favorite coffee shop in the world!), Oscar Cortez, Hingle McCringleberry, Jim Book, Tom Underwood, my Facebook friends, the staff and elders of

Journey Christian Church, and my church family—I'm still enjoying the journey and I really love you!

My favorite banjo-playing theologian, Ron Block—That lunch we shared in Nashville was a feast for my soul. Thanks for allowing me to share this book with you when it was nothing more than random thoughts on a napkin. Your excitement about this book at that early stage inspired me to get serious about writing it. Thank you.

My chiropractor, Dr. Brad Keeney—Thank you for adjusting my back and my view of discipleship. Your devotion to your patients, your Lord, and your family is inspirational.

Tammy Yoho—Thank you for sharing your son and his story with us. He will never be forgotten.

My readers—You can't know how much you mean to me. I wrote this book for you. I wouldn't trade you for all the readers in the world!

My Savior, Jesus Christ—Oh, how I love you!

ABOUT THE AUTHOR

ARRON CHAMBERS loves Jesus, his beautiful wife, his four wonderful children, and his church family at Journey Christian Church in Greeley, Colorado. He also loves coffee, Krispy Kreme donuts, sweet tea, worship music, cat videos, University of Tennessee football, Ridgewood Bar-B-Q, NASCAR, snowy mornings, Andrew Peterson music, Broadway musicals, Fontas Pizza, the Lexi, and chicken wings from the Wing Shack. But more than any of that and everything else, Arron's passion is communicating the love of Jesus through speaking and writing.

Other books by Arron:

Running on Empty: Life Lessons to Refuel Your Life

Scripture to Live By

Remember Who You Are!

Yendo Con El Tanque Vacío (Spanish Translation
of *Running on Empty*)

Go!

Eats with Sinners

Arron loves to hear from readers. You can write
Arron at *arron@arronchambers.com*.

For more information on Arron's ministry: *www.arronchambers.com*.

To check out Journey Christian Church: *www.enjoythejourney.us*.

For more about this book and for downloadable
resources: www.DevotedBook.com.

NOTES

CHAPTER 1: WAITING: TRUE LOVE WAITS

1. "True Love Waits Gifts & Merchandise," *Café Press*, accessed October 7, 2013, www.cafepress.com/+true-love-waits+gifts.

2. Yiren Lu, "Insanity: The Rise of the Supercharged Home Workout," *The Atlantic*, May 17, 2013, www.theatlantic.com/health/archive/2013/05/insanity-the-rise-of-the-supercharged-home-workout/275907/.

3. Khaled Hosseini, *A Thousand Splendid Suns* (New York: Riverhead Books, 2007), 126.

CHAPTER 3: SEEING: LOVE AT FIRST SIGHT

4. Alex, "Bird Poo Jesus," *The Museum of Hoaxes*, February 27, 2013, www.museumofhoaxes.com/hoax/weblog/comments/bird_poo_jesus.

5. Andy Campbell, "Dog Butt Looks Like Jesus Christ In A Robe (PHOTO)," *Huffington Post: Weird News*, June 14, 2013, www.huffingtonpost.com/2013/06/13/dog-butt-looks-like-jesus-photo_n_3436086.html.

6. Lee G. Healy, "Piece of cheese toast appears to feature the image of Jesus: Manna from heaven?" *GoUpstate.com*, April 22, 2009, www.goupstate.com/article/20090422/ARTICLES/904221068.

7. Brad Bromling, "What Does it Mean to Say Jesus is the 'Son of God'?" *Apologetics Press*, www.apologeticspress.org/apcontent.aspx?category=10&article=272.

8. Ray S. Anderson, "Son of God," *The International Standard Bible Encyclopedia*, vol. Q-Z, ed. Geoffrey W. Bromiley (Grand Rapids, Michigan: William B. Eerdmans Publishing Company, 1991), 571.

9. Brennan Manning, *The Furious Longing of God* (Colorado Springs, CO: David C. Cook, 2009), Kindle edition, 125.

CHAPTER 4: SPEAKING: TO TELL THE TRUTH

10. I want to thank all of my Facebook and Twitter friends for many of these suggestions. Also, more to my point, I'd recommend this video my friend, Todd Frenier, shared with me: "Shoot Christians Say," YouTube video, 2:13, posted by "Tripp and Tyler," May 30, 2013, www.youtube.com/watch?feature=player_embedded&v=7DxooYjno3I#at=61.

11. Dietrich Bonhoeffer, *Life Together* (San Francisco: Harper & Row Publishers, Inc., 1954), 107.

12. "907. Baptize," *Strong's Concordance* on BibleHub.com, http://biblehub.com/greek/907.htm, accessed 5/7/14.

CHAPTER 5: LEARNING: "A MIND IS A TERRIBLE THING TO WASTE"

13. David Sable, "'A Mind Is a Terrible Thing to Waste': An Iconic Campaign Turns 40," *Advertising Age*, March 3, 2011, adage.com/article/goodworks/a-mind-a-terrible-thing-waste-iconic-campaign-turns-40/149182/.

14. "100 Fascinating Facts You Never Knew About the Human Brain," *Nursing Assistant Central*, December 31, 2008, www.nursingassistantcentral.com/blog/2008/100-fascinating-facts-you-never-knew-about-the-human-brain/.

15. "Discipleship," Assemblies of God download, ag.org/discipleship_downloads/what_is_discipleship.pdf.

16. S. Michael Houdmann, "What is Christian discipleship?" *GotQuestions?org* www.gotquestions.org/Christian-discipleship.html.

17. "What is Discipleship: What is discipleship and what is Jesus calling us to in Matthew 28:18-20?" *Discipleship Tools*, www.discipleshiptools.org/pages.asp?pageid=65405.

18. James E. Faust, "Discipleship," The Church of Jesus Christ of Latter-day Saints, October 2006, www.lds.org/general-conference/2006/10/discipleship?lang=eng.

19. Janice Thompson, "Eight Keys to Discipling New Christians: Suggestions to help you mentor," *Christianity Today*, Spiritual Formation, February 18, 2004, www.christianitytoday.com/biblestudies/articles/spiritualformation/040218_2.html.

20. Some of the information in this section was influenced by an article by Dr. James E. Smith, "The Hands of the Apostles," Bible professor, miscellaneous lecture material pdf download, www.bibleprofessor.com/files/HandsApostles.pdf. For further information on this subject and the teaching ministry of Dr. E. James Smith, go to this site: www.bibleprofessor.com.

CHAPTER 6: SHARING: ON POUND CAKE–FILLED PURSES

21. C. S. Lewis, *The Screwtape Letters* (New York, New York: Collier Books, 1982), viii.

22. "Most American Christians Do Not Believe that Satan or the Holy Spirit Exist," *Barna Group: Knowledge to Navigate a Changing World*, April 10, 2009, www.barna.org/barna-update/article/12-faithspirituality/260-most-american-christians-do-not-believe-that-satan-or-the-holy-spirit-exis#.UheooxbnCbM.

23. Lewis, vii.

24. There are three major types of angelic beings mentioned in the Bible: seraphim, cherubim, and archangels, and up to seven more if you include: dominions, virtues, powers, thrones, principalities, angels, and demons.

25. According to this university's website, the only "lethal measure" for killing a snake is a long-handled shovel or a hoe. "Snake Control," NC State University, A&T State University Cooperative Extension, www.ces.ncsu.edu/gaston/Pests/reptiles/snakecontrol.htm. As noted, the heel of the Messiah is also lethal.

26 See 1 Samuel 14: 24-30; Matthew 6:16,17; Mark 2:18-20.

27. "Battle at Kruger," YouTube video, 8:24, posted by Jason Schlosberg, May 3, 2007, a www.youtube.com/watch?v=LU8DDYz68kM.

28. A "small group" is a name that is often used for a group of Christians who gather together frequently for Bible study, prayer, and . . . you guessed it. . . fellowship! If you aren't in a small group, I'd encourage you to look for one when you finish this period of waiting, or sooner if God leads you to one.

CHAPTER 7: REMEMBERING: THE DESCANSO AT MILE MARKER 38

29. In the town where I grew up, there's a church that offers drive-in worship. Here you go: "Drive-In Worship," Central Christian Church (Disciples of Christ), cccorlando.weebly.com/drive-in-worship.html.

30. For more information on eating with sinners, check out my book, Arron Chambers, *Eats with Sinners: Reaching Hungry People Like Jesus Did* (Cincinnati, Ohio: Standard Publishing, 2009).

31 Alexis De Tocqueville, translated by Henry Reeve, *Democracy in America, Volume 2* (A Public Domain Book, 2012), Kindle edition, 109-110.

32. Calvin Miller, *The Table of Inwardness: Nurturing Our Inner Life in Christ* (Downer's Grove, Illinois: Inter-Varsity Press, 1984), 36.

33. Miller, 35.

34 E.M. Bounds, *Purpose in Prayer: Enhanced Edition: Annotated & Illustrated* (Redemption Publishing, March 29, 2014), Kindle edition, 159.

35 Taken from a letter written to U.S. Senator Mark Hatfield as a response to his congratulatory letter to her upon her receipt of the Nobel Peace Prize. Published in *Major Addresses Delivered at the Conference on Faith and Learning* (North Newton, Bethel College, 1980), 85-86.

36. The first cup was the Cup of Sanctification remembering this promise, "I will bring you out from under the burdens of the Egyptians" (Exodus 6:6). The second cup was the Cup of Deliverance remembering this promise, "I will deliver you from slavery to them" (Exodus 6:6). The third cup was the Cup of Redemption remembering this promise, "I will redeem you with an outstretched arm" (Exodus 6:6). The fourth cup was the Cup of Restoration remembering this promise, "I will take you to be my people" (Exodus 6:7).

37. This heresy is known as Docetism, which has its roots in Greek Gnosticism and the belief that all flesh is "evil," therefore Jesus couldn't have had a "fleshly" body or he would have also been "evil."

38 Andrew Peterson, "Deliver Us," *Behold the Lamb of God* © 2004 Fervent Records. Used with permission.

CHAPTER 8: PRAYING: "I PLEDGE ALLIGIANCE"

39. Dietrich Bonhoeffer, *Life Together: A Discussion of Christian Fellowship* (San Francisco: Harper & Row Publishers, Inc., 1954), 47.

40. Mike Aquilina and Christopher Bailey, *Praying the Psalms with the Early Christians: Ancient Songs for Modern Hearts* (Frederick, Maryland: The Word Among Us Press, 2009), Kindle edition, "Introduction." 132.

41. Aguilina and Bailey, 132.

42. Thanks to my friend Sandy Daniel for this view of praying.

43. Joe Thomas, "John Bunyan: Mender of Pilgrim Souls," *Christianity.com*, www.christianity.com/church/church-history/notable-christians/john-bunyan -mender-of-pilgrim-souls-11630161.html.

44. John Brown, "John Bunyan: His Life, Times and Work" (London: J.B. Virtue and Co., Limited, 1885), 446, play.google.com/books/reader?prints ec=frontcover&output=reader&id=rAoMAQAAIAAJ&pg=GBS.PA446.

45. Jeff Tracy, "Why Leaders Pray," quote from G. Micheal Cocoris, *Evangelism: A Biblical Approach*, World Network of Prayer, www.wnop.org/ articles/365-why-leaders-pray.

CHAPTER 9: BELIEVING: LEAP!

46. Steve Scott, "How to Chain an Elephant: Breaking the Shackles We've Placed on Ourselves," guest post by Danny Iny, *Steve Scott Site: Internet Lifestyle Without the B.S.*, www.stevescottsite.com/how-to-chain-an-elephant.

47. "NASA Links," www.angelfire.com/ab/hotbot/nasa.html.

CHAPTER 10: SACRIFICING: "OR, BUY MYSELF A CAR!"

48. Maria Lianos-Carbone, "5 reasons why I don't force my kids to share: Why it's ok not to share some things when you're a kid," *Canadian Living: Moms*, www.canadianliving.com/moms/toddlers/5_reasons_why_i_dont _force_my_kids_to_share.php.

49 Booker T. Washington, *Up From Slavery: An Autobiography* (A Public Domain Book, 2012), Kindle edition, 4-5.

CHAPTER 11: ENJOYING: WAIST-DEEP IN UNEXPECTED JOY

50. Jason Samenow, "Colorado's 'biblical' flood by the numbers," *The Washington Post*, September 16, 2013, www.washingtonpost.com/blogs/ capital-weather-gang/wp/2013/09/16 /colorados-biblical-flood-by-the-numbers/.

51. "Statewide Flood Quick Facts: September 20 at 7:30 PM," Colorado Office of Emergency Management, September 20, 2013, www.coemergency.com/2013/09/statewide-flood-quick-facts -september_4407.html.

52. According to Strong's Concordance: agalliasis: exultation, exuberant joy
Original Word: ἀγαλλίασις, εως, ἡ
Part of Speech: Noun, Feminine
Transliteration: agalliasis
Phonetic Spelling: (ag-al-lee'-as-is)
Short Definition: exultation, exhilaration
Definition: wild joy, ecstatic delight, exultation, exhilaration.

53. Mahmud Faisal, "Arthur Ashe and An Explanation of Life," *Lights and Shadows: An attempt to enlighten my shadowed feelings*, June 19, 2010, expressionsunbound.wordpress.com/2010/06/19/ arthur-ashe-and-an-explanation-of-life/.

54 A famous catchphrase from the television show *Diff'rent Strokes* (1978-1986).
55 Eusebius, *History of the Church*, trans. Arthur Cushman McGiffert, (Acheron Press, November 5, 2012), Kindle edition, chapter 23:20.
56 Eusebius, chapter 23:10-18.

CHAPTER 12: PRAISING: SIX NICKELS AND THREE DIMES' WORTH OF WORSHIP

57. Everett Ferguson, *Early Christians Speak: Faith and life in the first three centuries,* revised ed. (Abilene, Texas: Biblical Research Press assigned to Abilene Christian University Press, 1987), 81. Quote taken from Pliny the Younger, *Letters: Addressed to the Emperor Trajan,* Book X.xcvi. The translation is that of William Melmoth in the Loeb Classical Library (Cambridge, Mass.: Harvard University Press, 1915).
58. Ferguson, 67–68, 81–82. Quote taken from Justin Martyr, *Apology* I, 67: 1–3, 7.
59. Jaroslav Pelikan, *The Vindication of Tradition: The 1983 Jefferson Lecture in the Humanities* (New Haven, Connecticut: Yale University, 1984), 65.
60. Dan Kimball, *Adventures in Churchland: Finding Jesus in the Mess of Organized Religion* (Grand Rapids, Michigan: Zondervan, 2012), 122.

CHAPTER 13: GROWING: THE MAGIC PILL

61. Based on the "Cost of Raising a Child" calculator on www.babycenter.com /cost-of-raising-child-calculator.
62. "Small Churches Struggle to Grow Because of the People They Attract," *Barna Group: Knowledge to navigate a changing world,* September 2, 2003, www.barna.org/barna-update/article/5-barna-update/126-small-churches -struggle-to-grow-because-of-the-people-they-attract#.Uk5kKOK2Dls. Introduction.
63. Barna, "Hope for Small Churches" in "Small Churches Struggle to Grow Because of the People They Attract."
64. Vanessa Covington, "Tea Party Dreams," *Bloom Right Here!* July 24, 2007, vanessacovington.blogspot.com/2007/07/tea-party-dreams.html.
65. Covington.
66. C. S. Lewis, *The Lion, the Witch and the Wardrobe: A Story for Children* (New York, New York: Macmillan Publishing Company, 1950), 75–76.

THE 40-DAY DEVOTED EXPERIENCE

67. Brennan Manning, *Abba's Child: The Cry of the Heart for Intimate Belonging* (Colorado Springs, CO: NavPress, 2002), 58.
68. "Battle at Kruger," YouTube video, 8:24, posted by Jason Schlosberg, May 3, 2007, www.youtube.com/watch?v=LU8DDYz68kM.

ACKNOWLEDGMENTS

69. Elie Wiesel, *Night,* trans. Marion Wiesel (New York: Hill and Wang, 2006), *xiv.*